Birding Arizona

By
Bill McMillon

FALCON™

Falcon Press ® Publishing Co., Inc.,
Helena, Montana

A **FALCON** GUIDE

Falcon Press is continually expanding its list of recreational guidebooks. All books include detailed descriptions, accurate maps, and all information necessary for enjoyable trips. You can order extra copies of this book and get information and prices for other Falcon guidebooks by writing Falcon Press, P.O. Box 1718, Helena, MT 59624 or calling toll-free 1-800-582-2665. Also, please ask for a free copy of our current catalog.

© 1995 by Falcon Press Publishing Co., Inc.,
Helena and Billings, Montana.

Printed in the United States of America

Front and back cover photos: Stephen and Michele Vaughan
All black-and-white photos by author

♻ Text pages printed on recycled paper.

ISBN: 1-56044-230-1

Library of Congress Cataloging-in-Publication Data

McMillon, Bill, 1942-
    Birding Arizona / Bill McMillon.
        p.   cm.
    Includes bibliographical references (p.   ) and index.
    ISBN 1-56044-230-1 (pbk.)
        1. Bird watching—Arizona—Guidebooks. 2. Arizona—Guidebooks.
    I. Title.
    QL683.A6M35 1996
    598'.07234791-95; jb08 01-05-96; jb02 01-17-96—dc20   96-380
                                                                      CIP

CAUTION

Outdoor recreation activities are by their very nature potentially hazardous. All participants in such activities must assume the responsibility for their own actions and safety. The information contained in this guidebook cannot replace sound judgment and good decision–making skills, which help reduce risk exposure, nor does the scope of this book allow for disclosure of all the potential hazards and risks involved in such activities.

Learn as much as possible about the outdoor recreation activities you participate in, prepare for the unexpected, and be safe and cautious. The reward will be a safer and more enjoyable experience.

This book is for my brother Ray,
who helped nourish a seminal interest
in birdwatching and nature.

Acknowledgments

Many authors mention that they could not have written a book without the help given by others. This book is truly one that could never have been finished without the information freely given by dozens of life birders who took time out from their search for new birds for the life list to give this birding novice assistance.

Though I have been a bird watcher since childhood, I have done so only casually. I had picked up plenty of information along the line, but I was not prepared for the daunting task that I undertook as I began this guide to Arizona. Only a life birder would have been, and I found that most of these are far too busy researching their next trip to compile a guide.

The guide would never have been completed, therefore, without the assistance provided by Russ Agnew and Mike Heffernon, very serious life birders who helped me as I struggled along, and the many unnamed birders I encountered along the trail as I crossed the state.

I must also commend John Grassy, whose patience was sorely tried as I endured serious doubts about ever completing the guide and procrastinated beyond reason. He kept his calm, most of the time, when I failed to return his calls or meet my deadlines. Thank you, John.

Contents

Acknowledgments.. iii

Introduction.. vii

How to use this guide viii

Chapter 1. Planning an Arizona birding trip

When to go birding.. 1

What to wear 1

Essentials for a successful birding trip 2

Where to stay... 2

Field hazards 3

An ethical approach to birding 5

Maps 5

Birding organizations 6

Chapter 2. Arizona's habitats

The Arizona landscape 7

Topography 7

Climate 8

Vegetation.. 8

Birds of Arizona's regions 10

Seasons 12

Migrations 12

Map legend 14

Chapter 3. Arizona's best birding areas

Arizona map 15

Northern Arizona: Canyonlands and plateaus

Regional map... 17

1. Mount Trumbull area 18

2. North Rim and Kaibab Plateau Parkway 20

3. Aubrey Valley 22

4. Coleman Lake...24

5. White Horse Lake and Pine Flat route 25

6. Grandview Point and Forest Road 302 loop 27

7. Red Butte and Red Mountain loop 29

8. Lamar Haines Memorial Wildlife Area 31

9. Mormon Lake area 33

10. Petrified Forest drive 35

Western Arizona: Rivers and deserts

Regional map 37

11. Hualapai Mountain Park and Wabayuma Peak Wilderness 39

12. Bill Williams Delta National Wildlife Refuge, Bill Williams Gorge,
and Alamo Lake State Park 41

13. Kofa National Wildlife Refuge 44

14. Imperial National Wildlife Refuge and Martinez Lake 47

15. Mittry Lake and Betty's Kitchen 50

16. Hassayampa River Preserve and Burro Creek 51

17. Organ Pipe Cactus National Monument 54

Central Arizona: Mountains

Regional map 59

18. Dead Horse Ranch State Park and Tuvasci Marsh 60

19. Red Rock State Park 62

20. Tonto Natural Bridge State Park 63

21. Canyon Creek and Tonto Creek Recreation Area 64

22. Verde River and Horseshoe Dam 66

23. Phon D. Sutton Recreation Area 69

24. Fish Creek and Roosevelt Lake Wildlife Area 71

25. Allen Severson Wildlife Area and Jacques Marsh 73

26. Springerville and Big Lake loop 75

27. Escudilla Mountain and Terry Flat 77

28. Eagle Creek and Honeymoon Campground 79

29. Bonita Creek 81

Southeastern Arizona: Sky Islands

Regional map 83

30. Aravaipa Canyon 85

31. Catalina State Park 87

32. Sabino Canyon Recreation Area 89

33. Mount Lemmon drive 90

34. Saguaro National Monument 91

35. Arizona-Sonora Desert Museum 92
36. Buenos Aires National Wildlife Refuge 94
37. Madera Canyon and Florida Wash 97
38. Patagonia Sonoita Creek Preserve 100
39. San Pedro Riparian National Conservation Area 101
40. Ramsey Canyon and Carr Canyon 103
41. Willcox Playa Wildlife Area 105
42. Guadalupe Canyon 107
43. Cave Creek Canyon and Rustler Park 108
44. Empire/Cienega Resource Conservation Area 110
45. Sycamore Canyon Loop 111

**Chapter 4. Checklist, seasonal occurrence,
and abundance of Arizona birds** 113

Chapter 5. Arizona bird specialties 151

Appendix I: Reporting rare bird information 184
Appendix II: Arizona birding organizations 187
Appendix III: Agency index 188
Appendix IV: American Birding Association Code of Ethics 196

Bibliography
Selected readings on Arizona birds 198
Birding Magazines 199

Index 200

Introduction

Arizona, particularly the Sky Islands in the southeastern part of the state, is a birder's mecca. And well it should be, with more than 480 species of birds having been reported within the state. Few other states offer the variety of habitats, the closeness to Mexico (from which many avian migrants cross over into the lower sections of Arizona), or the location along many migration routes that bring so many species to Arizona.

When I was asked to write this guide I couldn't pass up the opportunity to spend more time in search of Elegant Trogon, Masked Bobwhite (a rare subspecies of Northern Bobwhite), Mexican Chickadee, Crested Caracara, and dozens of other birds that birders from around the world come to see.

From the Sky Islands of southeastern Arizona, where I began my research, I headed to the sparse desert lands of southwestern Arizona, and then continued north along the Colorado River to the high plateaus and deep canyons of northern Arizona before finally ending in the mountains of central Arizona.

Of these regions, only southeastern Arizona had guidebooks published about birding sites, and that is because the Sky Islands and surrounding grasslands are where most of the unusual birds of the state can be found. I discovered abundant birding sites in the other portions of the state, however, and hope this book will guide birders to spots such as the Kofa National Wildlife Refuge, Organ Pipe Cactus National Monument, and Imperial National Wildlife Refuge. It may even draw you to the isolated Uinkaret and Shivwits plateaus above the North Rim of the Grand Canyon, places few people explore.

I didn't shortchange the great birding areas of southeastern Arizona, though, in my efforts to give the rest of the state its due. There was no way I was going to miss birding again in the grasslands of Buenos Aires National Wildlife Refuge, in the riparian growth of the San Pedro Riparian National Conservation Area, or in the most wonderful areas of all, the Chiricahua, Santa Rita, and Huachuca mountains, small ranges that rise from the surrounding high desert.

As you dream of spotting that new bird only seen in Arizona, use this guide to help you make those dreams a reality, and remember, there is more to Arizona birding than visiting the Sky Islands in the southeastern portion of the state.

How to use this guide

This guide was written to give birders, both residents and visitors to Arizona, one resource to the best places to see and hear birds in the diverse habitats of this large state. It does not pretend to be the definitive work on all the birds of the state, nor does it attempt to be a field guide to identifying birds. It makes no attempt to be comprehensive; rather, its intent is to provide for the first time a birding guide that covers all the state's regions. The book is sort of a road map of where to go throughout the state to find good birding. In addition to identifying the best birding spots in the state, it provides details on the natural history of the regions where the birds congregate. Serious birders can use it to map out their itineraries as they head for Arizona to locate rare birds, and novices can use it to begin their quest for good birding sites where they are sure to see and hear a number of Arizona's beautiful birds.

For both experienced and novice birders I recommend using the Recreational Map of Arizona (GTR Mapping, P.O. Box 1984, Canon City, CO 81215-1984; (719) 275-8948) when organizing trips. This map was developed for outdoor enthusiasts of all types, and includes information about more than 300 recreational sites around the state. The map is available at bookstores and tourists spots throughout the state, or you can order it directly from the publisher. The Arizona Office of Tourism offers an official Arizona Department of Transportation highway map, as well as a number of other travel guides to the state. You can obtain these by contacting the Arizona Office of Tourism, 1100 W. Washington, Phoenix, AZ 85007; (602) 542-8087.

Chapter 1 of this guide covers all the information essential to a successful birding trip to the state. This includes information on when to go, what to wear, a checklist of essentials, where to stay, hazards likely to be encountered in the field, and birding ethics. Names of various birding organizations in the state are also included. There are more of these in Appendix III.

Chapter 2 gives readers information about the many habitats found in Arizona, from the low deserts to the high plateaus. Environmental factors that affect bird distribution such as topography, climate, and vegetation are described briefly.

Chapter 3 identifies Arizona's best birding areas. Forty-five sites from four regions are described here. These diverse regions begin with the canyonlands of northern Arizona, then move to the Colorado River and Sonoran Desert regions of western and southern Arizona before covering the central Mountains. The last region, the Sky Islands of southeastern Arizona, is one of the top five birding spots in all of North America.

The Arizona Bird Committee has defined three major avifaunal regions in Arizona (Northern, Southwestern, and Southeastern), which overlap to some extent. I have taken part of the Northern Region, added the overlap of the three regions, and formed a fourth region, which I call the Central Mountains.

Birding is a year-round activity in Arizona, but spring and fall are the best times for most of the state. A word for people from regions of the country where spring begins sometime between mid-April and early June: Spring comes early in Arizona. In the low deserts of the southwest portion of the state the first signs of spring appear by late February, and spring is in full force all across southern Arizona by mid-March. So please don't head for Arizona in late May and early June and expect to see spring birds. Only along the Colorado River in the far southwest and along the southern edges of the Sonoran Desert is birding good to excellent in the winter, and summer birding is moderate in the higher elevations of the state. Many species winter along the Colorado and in the many lakes formed along it before they begin their migration back north as spring comes.

Each site description provides quick details of the site so you can determine what birds are found there without reading the entire text. The site names are printed in boldface, and birds generally found there are listed together and grouped by preferred habitat. Each entry has introductory material that highlights what is found there, a more detailed text of birding information, a map or maps, and helpful information about the region, including where to find food, lodging, camping, and gas, plus where to obtain more information about the area.

The maps for each entry are best used along with the Recreation Map of Arizona, The Arizona Atlas and Gazetteer (DeLorme Mapping, P.O. Box 298, Freeport, ME 04032; (207) 865-4171), USDAFS and BLM maps, and USGS topographical maps.

Chapter 4 is the Checklist of the Birds of Arizona compiled by the Arizona Bird Committee. This list includes details of seasonal and relative abundance of the birds found in the state.

Chapter 5 provides more in-depth information on 125 birds that are representative of Arizona habitats, many of which are much sought after by birders from around the world.

This is followed by Appendices I through IV. Appendix I tells how to report rare bird sightings. Appendix II is a listing of Arizona birding organizations. Appendix III is a listing of governmental and nonprofit agencies who own or administer land where birders may go to seek new sightings, and Appendix IV is the American Birding Association Code of Ethics. This is followed by a list of sources for further reading.

Planning an Arizona birding trip

When to go birding

Anytime is a good time to go birding in Arizona. It just depends upon where you are and when you want to head out. The higher levels of the Sky Islands are covered with snow in midwinter, as are the Central Mountains and high plateaus, but the high desert grasslands of the southeastern portion of the state, the Sonoran Desert area around Tucson and south of Phoenix, the deserts of the southwestern portion of the state, and the Colorado River region are all warm, and have plenty of birds at that time.

Spring, after the snow and cold nights have left, is the best time to head for the Sky Islands and the Central Mountains, and the lower deserts are still pleasant. Birds are plentiful during this time, since migrants are on the move and those birds that nest in the region are beginning their courtships. Summer drives most people, and birds, out of the low desert regions, and both head for the higher elevations where the temperatures are pleasant and, for birds, the foraging is good. This is the time to explore the high canyonlands and plateaus, the Central Mountains, and the higher slopes of the Sky Islands.

Fall is a good time to head for the low deserts, lower slopes of the Sky Islands, and the grasslands of the high desert to watch for fall migrants as they head for Mexico and points south. Waterfowl also begin to congregate along the Colorado River at this time.

What to wear

Location as well as season affects what you want to wear. During summer you can get by with minimal amounts of clothing except at the highest elevations, and you certainly want to have few clothes on your body in the heat of midsummer in the low deserts. In spring and fall, nights and early mornings can be cool to cold even in the low deserts; in winter, be prepared for cold anywhere you go in the state.

One item to always wear in the sunny Southwest is a hat. The sun beats down incessantly, and without a hat your eyes become useless and your head heats to the point you wish you were anywhere but birding. You should also wear plenty of sunscreen, since Arizona is part of what has been called "the cancer-belt."

Many birding areas are covered with a layer of rock, much of it volcanic in origin, so sturdy hiking shoes or boots are a good idea when you plan to spend any time on the trail. Along with the sturdy boots, you should be sure your socks are heavy enough to protect you from blisters, but not so heavy as to cause excess sweating in hot weather.

Raingear is another necessity. Although we think of the desert as a dry place (and it is), storms do cross the higher elevations with regularity during much of the year, and summer is monsoon season in the Southwest. Afternoon downpours come with almost clockwork timing each day, and often fall during prime birding times in early morning and late evening.

Although not technically clothing, one item that you always want to have with your clothing is a good-sized water bottle or bag. Many of the outings in this guide are into dry areas where there is no source of water. Hiking in the dry climate of Arizona quickly leads to dehydration any time of the year.

Essentials for a successful birding trip

The following is a checklist of items essential for a good birding trip anywhere, but especially in Arizona, where some sites are far from civilization.

_____ highway map or maps

_____ USGS topographical, USDAFS, BLM, and local site maps

_____ good-quality binoculars and scopes

_____ field identification guides for region

_____ sunscreen and insect repellent

_____ toilet paper and trowel or Ziploc bag

_____ drinking water (both in vehicle and on the trail)

_____ ice chest for keeping water and other drinks cool

_____ food for snacking

_____ field journal

_____ camera and film

_____ first-aid kit

_____ extra money

_____ camping equipment if exploring more isolated sites

_____ a compatible companion

Where to stay

Be prepared to camp if you head to Arizona for birding. Although some of the sites in this guide, maybe even a majority, are near populated areas where you can find adequate boarding and lodging, most of the best spots are quite a distance from these conveniences.

For birders, who like to be out on the trail in time for early morning bird activities, this means that you either have to rise extremely early to reach the good birding sites, or you camp near them. This is easy to do in Arizona with its abundance of public lands where you can camp even if there is no campground nearby. If you are choosy, and prefer to camp in developed campgrounds, even that is easy. Most of the great sites are within national forest lands, and developed campgrounds are scattered throughout these. State park campgrounds are also available near many of the sites.

You can obtain brochures on camping and lodging facilities, as well as maps and other travel guides, by contacting the Arizona Office of Tourism, 1100 W. Washington Street, Phoenix, AZ 85007; (602) 542-8087.

If you choose to do primitive camping, please take pride in leaving your campsite as clean or cleaner than you found it. Since trash cans and restroom facilities are not available you should always pack out all your garbage and bury all excrement and toilet paper at least 6 inches deep and 200 feet from any water supply or surface water.

Field hazards

Field hazards in Arizona are commonly thought to be heat, dehydration, and poisonous animals that attack the unwary. While there is some truth to these hazards (I will cover them a bit later), the hazard that is most likely to cause problems for visitors to the wildlands of Arizona is hypothermia. Yes, hypothermia. Since people are so concerned about the heat, they forget about the cold and are unprepared for summer thunderstorms that soak anything not covered, cold desert nights, and general cold conditions found at the higher elevations of the state. A little-known fact is that more people die of hypothermia in Arizona each year than they do of thirst and heat prostration combined. You can even add those killed from venomous bites and still have fewer than those killed by cold and wet conditions.

Not that you should ignore the problems of heat and thirst, for they are real. It is inadvisable to head out on the trail for extended periods in the heat of midsummer, and one should always carry a container of water while on the trail. Thirst comes quickly in the low humidity of Arizona, and people do become dehydrated, even in cool weather.

Nor should you ignore the problems presented by rattlesnakes, scorpions, and other venomous creatures that crawl along the desert floor. These creatures generally avoid humans, but you may find yourself face-to-face with a rattlesnake as you explore a wash or walk through cactus-covered desert. If you do, simply back away and give it plenty for room to slither into its own safe place. Rattlesnakes only attack large mammals when threatened. Even if you are bitten, don't panic. Few deaths occur from a single rattlesnake bite. Relax; slowly walk back to your vehicle and have a companion drive you to the nearest hospital. You will encounter considerable pain, but you are unlikely to die.

Scorpions are a little different. They don't attack, but they do hide in cool, protected places, such as sleeping bags and boots, and will bite as a defense if they are not removed. Before you put on a piece of clothing, slip into your sleeping bag, or insert your feet into your boots, shake them sharply. Any scorpions that have hidden there will fall out and scurry away.

Much more hazardous, although seldom life-threatening, are the sticky and prickly plants that thrive in the hot deserts. From jumping cholla to mesquite trees, just about every plant in the desert has spines or thorns. These can cause severe discomfort, and may even require minor surgery to be removed, if you come into too close contact with them. The spines of jumping cholla seemingly "jump" off the plants when you only have minimal contact, and the fishhook-shaped, barbed spines become deeply embedded in your skin. Other spines and thorns also break off easily as you are stuck, and become deeply embedded with minimal contact. Getting the spines and thorns out hurts, and when either breaks off beneath the skin they can cause infections.

The message here is BE CAREFUL. Wear good boots (sneakers offer very little protection), long pants, and long sleeves when walking among the prickly plants. And watch where you are going.

As strange as it may seem, water is also a real hazard in desert country. What was a dry wash on a clear day can become a roaring river of mud, water, and boulders with only a moment's notice. Thunderstorms far away can drop buckets of water that become flash floods miles downstream where you may be completely unaware of any problem. This is especially true at night. For this reason, never camp in the low spots of a dry wash. Move up to higher ground along its banks. Even during the day you should know how to get out of any wash where you are hiking in case you hear the roaring of a flash flood coming down it.

Cars, desert roads, and dry washes can also make a lethal combination. If you do drive off highway onto one of the many dirt roads of Arizona, be careful. Although the roads are generally safe, there are some hazards you must watch out for. Be extremely cautious about crossing dry washes. There may be deep sand and you may get stuck, even with a four-wheel-drive vehicle. (Edward Abbey once said that you were in trouble if you really needed your four-wheel drive. He argued that you could go as far with a two-wheel drive pickup as you needed to—any farther, you should walk.) Don't drive on dirt roads as though they were city streets. Although many are well-maintained, others are only slightly so and provide plenty of road hazards for those driving too fast. Also, be careful not to park your vehicle in a wash as you head out birding. Find a high place just in case. Flash floods are not frequent, but when they do happen you want to have your vehicle on high ground.

Most hazards of birding in Arizona are minor, but even those that can be life-threatening can be minimized with some thought and preparation. Be prepared for both heat and cold on any extended outing. Always have a good supply of water, both at your base camp and on the trail. Always be on the lookout for plants and animals that stick, prick, sting, hook, or tear. Always be aware that water can roar down low spots such as washes with little or no notice. Always treat the desert and dry high-country as an "enemy" that you have to keep an eye out for. Follow these simple precautions and you will avoid most of the hazards found in the outdoors of Arizona.

An ethical approach to birding

A popular children's cartoon character tells her pets that she is going to "love them, squeeze them, and never let them go." Though birders are not likely to follow her actions, there is, nevertheless, a bit of this character in all of us who enjoy wild creatures. As we search them out for our pleasure, we infringe upon their natural spaces, sometimes to the extent of harming their chances of surviving, much less thriving.

Outdoor recreation is increasing dramatically in all regions of Arizona, and this puts pressure on all types of wildlife. Birders and their organizations have become aware of our environmental impacts, and therefore make attempts to avoid disturbing birds or their habitats. This is a constant war, though, as more and more people become interested in birding. Novices are often unaware of how they can destroy a nesting site or disturb birds during critical breeding periods. As birders, part of our ongoing efforts must be to ensure that newcomers to birding are educated about how to watch birds without disturbing them.

Many recreational activities such as birding sometimes lead participants over the boundaries between public and private lands. While this may seem a trivial point to some who are more used to the definite boundaries one finds in urban and suburban areas, we must develop a mindset that says private land boundaries are important. We must maintain a sense of privacy in our pursuit of birds.

The following tips will help relieve the pressures placed on our wildlands and prevent territorial problems with private landowners:

1. The welfare of birds and other wildlife is above our desires as observers.

2. Respect the privacy of others, obtain permission before entering private property, and always leave gates and fences as you found them.

3. Keep your distance. If your presence provokes a change in the behavior of a bird or other wild animal, you are too close. Use high-powered scopes, binoculars, and/or telescopic lenses to avoid disturbing birds and animals.

4. Never disturb nesting birds, and avoid getting between parents and chicks.

5. Do not use artificial devices (such as recordings and bird calls) to attract birds. Find them using your own skill.

6. See the American Birding Association Code of Ethics (Appendix IV).

Maps

Always have a good Arizona road map handy. This can be a Recreation Map of Arizona from GTR Mapping, P.O. Box 1984, Canon City, CO 81215-1984; (719) 275-8948, or an official Arizona Department of Transportation map from the Arizona Office of Tourism, 1100 W. Washington Street, Phoenix, AZ 85007; (602) 542-8087.

U.S. government agencies such as the Bureau of Land Management and the USDA Forest Service provide maps of their lands. You can contact agencies noted in Appendix III for a listing of their maps for Arizona. These maps have more details on dirt roads in a region than regular highway maps provide.

The U.S. Geological Survey offers an assortment of maps covering Arizona. These can be obtained from outdoor equipment shops throughout the state, or by contacting the USGS, Denver Federal Center, Lakewood, CO 80225. You can request an index and price list of all maps that cover Arizona.

Birding organizations

American Birding Association

For serious birders, one organization stands out above all others. This is the nonprofit American Birding Association. The ABA is dedicated to all aspects of birding, and publishes a magazine and newsletter. For further information contact the American Birding Association, P.O. Box 6599, Colorado Springs, CO 80934; (800) 634-7736.

Audubon Society

Birders interested in Arizona birding specifically should contact any of the eight Arizona Audubon Chapters (see Appendix II) for local information.

Of these chapters, one is worth a further mention. The Tucson Audubon Society is one of the most active in the country, and in addition to normal chapter activities operates an excellent bookstore in Tucson, maintains a Birding Hotline, and conducts workshops that are attended by people nationwide.

Each of the chapters conducts field trips, Breeding Bird Surveys, and Christmas Bird Counts. The latter are a great way to learn about the birds of the area, and you are invited to contact the local chapter where you would like to participate. The CBC takes place sometime in the last two weeks of December and first two weeks of January each year.

Arizona Rare Bird Alert

To find out about recent bird sightings or to report a rare bird, contact either of the two Birding Hotlines in Arizona. Phoenix: (602) 832-8745; Tucson: (520) 798-1005.

CHAPTER 2 —————————————————————

Arizona's habitats

The Arizona landscape

Arizona is best known for its mighty deserts. Parts of four deserts—the Sonoran, Mojave, Great Basin, and Chiricahuan—reach into the state, and together they cover almost half its land. Despite their prominence, deserts are only one part of a complex landscape. It seems less accurate to think of Arizona's landscape as a single type, and more realistic to see it as an interlacing of deserts, mountains, and canyons, all of which can be found in every section of the state.

Even in the most torpid regions of southwestern Arizona where the Sonoran and Mojave deserts exert their mighty hold, mountains rise from the flat desert to form high desert, much of which is little different from the lower desert around it. These rocky islands receive little more rainfall than the surrounding desert, and offer little in terms of vegetation not found below.

As you head east in the Sonoran Desert, however, the mountains rise higher, and lush stands of pine and oak forests cover their slopes. There, the environment of the Sky Islands attracts hundreds of species of birds that find the varied habitats inviting.

Heading north into the central highlands of Arizona, you find the largest unbroken stand of ponderosa pine in the world north of the Mogollon Rim, a 2,000-foot escarpment that divides the low desert from the higher Colorado Plateau. This plateau has its own mountain ranges that rise from the mile-high flatlands of the plateau, as well as canyons. Everywhere you go you find canyons eroded through the vast sandstone plateau to depths of up to a mile, where the climate and landscape is much like that of the low desert far to the south.

All of these features—the four deserts, the Sky Islands, the Central Highlands, canyons, and plateaus—combine to provide as great a range of plants and animals found in any state in the union.

Topography

A topographical map of Arizona is marked by large expanses with no elevation changes suddenly broken by deep canyons or high peaks that abruptly drop or rise from the level regions of low desert. From the Colorado River in the north and along the western boundary of the state, the Sonoran and Mojave deserts are a series of large, open expanses broken by sharply jutting mountain ranges.

In the northern section of the state the land gently rises from the Colorado to form the plateaus that cover all of the lands beyond the Grand Canyon to the New Mexico border. There, in what is known as Red Rock country, canyons cut though the plateaus along the Little Colorado River and its tributaries, most seasonal, to form dramatic breaks in an otherwise flat landscape.

The White Mountains rise gently to the south of the plateau in the east-central part of the state to peaks more than 12,000 feet high. These collect significant rainfall during both summer and winter and nourish some of the most lush flora in Arizona.

In southeast Arizona a series of small mountain ranges jut up from high desert where grasslands often replace cactus forests. These collect significant rainfall during both summer and winter as they push rain clouds upward until they drop their moisture. The thick forests of pine and oak on the higher reaches of the range provide homes to a variety of wildlife.

Climate

Deserts, by definition, are dry, and those of Arizona are certainly no exception. The Sonoran, not as dry as the other three deserts in the state, is moderately wet for a desert, yet its rainfall ranges only from about 7.5 inches a year near Phoenix to over 11 inches a year in Tucson. This makes for good desert plant growth, which survives year-round below 3,000 feet since there are few freezing lows each year. Tucson, which is at about 2,000 feet, averages only seventeen such days a year, and then only a few degrees below the freezing point. Conversely, temperatures almost always reach above 100 degrees Fahrenheit during the day after mid-April or early May.

The temperatures are even higher in the far southwest portions of the state and north along the Colorado River, and even in the winter you seldom see below-freezing temperatures there.

The high plateau region of Northern Arizona is cooler, and although summer days may reach above 100 degrees, winters bring temperatures that are among the lowest in the nation, along with significant snowfall.

The Central Mountains are cooler still, with summer highs in the 80s and heavy snowpacks in the winter.

In southeastern Arizona there are more contrasts with the low desert and Sky Islands standing side by side. A wide range of temperatures and rainfall can occur within several miles. In fact, a good rule of thumb in most of Arizona is to expect the temperature to drop 3 to 4 degrees for every 1,000-foot gain in elevation and the average yearly precipitation to increase about 4 to 5 inches. This causes extreme variations in and around the Sky Island region where the ranges may climb 5,000 to 8,000 feet in 20 miles.

Vegetation

Biologists have assigned as many as six distinct life zones to Arizona's varied landscape, though they don't always agree on the names and boundaries of these.

Arizona's elevation ranges from below 2,000 feet along the lower Colorado River to over 13,000 feet in the San Francisco Peaks north of Flagstaff, and the difference between the vegetation of the two extremes is vast—so vast that, when the Mount Lemmon Road outside of Tucson was constructed to the top of Mount Lemmon in the 1930s, it was touted as "the road that could take you from Mexico to Canada in an hour." The Sky Islands of Southeastern Arizona don't have all the plant communities found in the state, but the region does have some representatives of the six important life zones.

Desert Scrub is found between 2,000 and 3,500 feet (610-1,067 m), and is generally an extension of the plant and animal communities found on the desert floor through the southern part of the state. A little higher rainfall and generous runoff from the higher slopes makes the vegetation, which is primarily forests of saguaro, mesquite, and paloverde, a little more lush than that found on the flat plains away from the ranges. In wet years there is a beautiful display of wildflowers on the open desert floor throughout the state.

Chaparral grows between 3,500 and 6,000 feet (1,067 and 1,829 m) in a temperate zone with tall grasses and tough-leafed shrubs such as manzanita. One potentially dangerous plant that rises above the chaparral is the self-descriptive "shindagger" agave.

Oak Woodlands dominate between 4,500 and 6,000 feet (1,372-1,829 m) in areas that get a little more moisture than that needed by chaparral. These are not dense forests, but scattered Emory oak, with some Arizona and Mexican oak mixed in, that grow from expanses of grassland except in riparian areas where the trees become denser.

Pinyon-juniper Woodlands are found from 5,000 to 7,000 feet (1,524-2,134 m) where substantial snow falls. The small, gnarled pinyon pine provides abundant nuts for large communities of birds including the Clark's Nutcracker, a jay that has developed a special pouch under its tongue for holding nuts. One nutcracker was found with ninety-five pinon nuts in its pouch.

Ponderosa Pine Forests grow at 7,000 to 9,000 feet (2,134-2,743 m). These are true forests dominated by the gigantic ponderosa. These trees reach as high as 125 feet and live for 200 to 400 years. The world's largest stand of this tree surrounds the San Francisco Peaks area of Northern Arizona, but it also grows in the higher elevations of the White Mountains and the Sky Islands.

Above 7,500 feet (2,286 m) you encounter the *Canadian Life Zone*, with its dark forests of Douglas-fir, white fir, and quaking aspen. The most notable stands of this forest are found on the slopes of the San Francisco Peaks, but there are also several sites in the White Mountains.

Probably the most important vegetation type in Arizona for birders is one that occurs at all elevations, and is dependent upon a steady water source rather than on change in elevation. *Riparian forests* grow along small streams and large rivers and around ponds and lakes throughout the state. Whether in the low desert, on the slopes of the Sky Islands, or near high mountain meadows, stands of willow, cottonwood, sycamore, and oak thrive near the dependable sources of water. Birds congregate in large numbers in these habitats, and some of the most productive birding in the state is found in sites such as the San Pedro Riparian National Conservation Area and Hassayampa River Preserve. Wherever you are in the state, you are more likely to spot birds in riparian forests than any other spot.

The identification of the small ranges that rise above the surrounding desert in southeastern Arizona as Sky Islands is apt. The long stretches of desert that ring these small ranges keep plants and animals isolated from others of the same species much in the same way vast expanses of ocean do, and many subspecies have evolved in the ranges over the millennia. Today, you can find subspecies of mammals and plants on just about every small peak in the southeastern portion of the state. One, the Mount Graham red squirrel, became the subject of a dispute over the ecological effects of the construction of a new astronomical observatory on top of Mount Graham, and construction was halted as the status of this sub-species was determined by wildlife biologists. At last report, construction of the observatory was moving forward, but conservationists are still fighting to halt it.

Birds of Arizona's regions

Since the habitats of Arizona are so varied, the birds found in them are vastly different. Though you seldom find good congregations of waterfowl in southeastern Arizona, you can readily find them along the Colorado River in the western part of the state. Greater Roadrunners don't appear in cold regions of the northern plateaus, but they can be see in abundance in the low deserts. There are dozens more of such examples.

Below are some of the more interesting birds you are likely to find in the three avifaunal regions of Arizona as defined by the Arizona Bird Committee. The birds of the fourth region that I have defined for this guide, the Central Mountains, come from the three regions defined below.

Southeastern Region

Wood Stork
Mallard
Mexican Duck
Redhead
Mississippi Kite
White-tailed (Black-shouldered) Kite
Northern Harrier
Harris' Hawk
Gray Hawk
Zone-tailed Hawk
Merlin
Montezuma Quail
Scaled Quail
Solitary Sandpiper
Willet
Spotted Sandpiper
Franklin's Gull
Forster's Tern
Inca Dove
White-winged Dove
Greater Roadrunner
Flammulated Owl
Whiskered Screech-Owl
Elf Owl
Short-eared Owl
Lesser Nighthawk
Common Nighthawk
Buff-collared Nightjar
Whip-poor-will
Broad-billed Hummingbird
Violet-crowned Hummingbird
Blue-throated Hummingbird
Magnificent Hummingbird
Allen's Hummingbird
Elegant Trogon
Belted Kingfisher
Green Kingfisher
Gila Woodpecker
Ladder-backed Woodpecker
Hairy Woodpecker

Strickland's Woodpecker
Northern Beardless-Tyrannulet
Buff-breasted Flycatcher
Black Phoebe
Dusky-capped Flycatcher
Sulphur-bellied Flycatcher
Tropical Kingbird
Thick-billed Kingbird
Gray-breasted Jay
Chihuahuan Raven
Mexican Chickadee
Bridled Titmouse
Cactus Wren
Eastern Bluebird
Bendire's Thrasher
Curve-billed Thrasher
Crissal Thrasher
LeConte's Thrasher
Hutton's Vireo
Grace's Warbler
Kentucky Warbler
Painted Redstart
Olive Warbler
Hepatic Tanager
Summer Tanager
Scarlet Tanager
Pyrrhuloxia
Blue Grosbeak
Varied Bunting
Abert's Towhee
Botteri's Sparrow
Cassin's Sparrow
Rufous-winged Sparrow
Baird's Sparrow
Grasshopper Sparrow
Yellow-eyed Junco
McCown's Longspur
Bronzed Cowbird

Southwestern Region

Western Grebe
Cattle Egret
Roseate Spoonbill
Gadwall
Greater Scaup
Common Goldeneye

Bufflehead
Hooded Merganser
Black Vulture
Turkey Vulture
Harris' Hawk
Gambel's Quail
Black Rail
Clapper Rail
Virginia Rail
Sandhill Crane
Mountain Plover
Black-necked Stilt
American Avocet
Greater Yellowlegs
Sanderling
Long-billed Dowitcher
Herring Gull
Caspian Tern
Common Tern
Yellow-billed Cuckoo
Anna's Hummingbird
Costa's Hummingbird
Vermilion Flycatcher
Ash-throated Flycatcher
Tree Swallow
Verdin
Cactus Wren
Marsh Wren
Black-tailed Gnatcatcher
Common Yellowthroat
Northern Cardinal
Yellow-headed Blackbird
Great-tailed Grackle
Brown-headed Cowbird

Northern Region

Eared Grebe
Mallard
Sharp-shinned Hawk
Northern Goshawk
Swainson's Hawk
Ferruginous Hawk
Chukar
Ring-necked Pheasant
Blue Grouse
Wild Turkey

Montezuma Quail
Scaled Quail
Killdeer
Spotted Sandpiper
Common Snipe
Band-tailed Pigeon
Flammulated Owl
Northern Pygmy-Owl
Spotted Owl
Northern Saw-whet Owl
Lewis' Woodpecker
Acorn Woodpecker
Yellow-bellied Sapsucker
Hairy Woodpecker
Three-toed Woodpecker
Northern Yellow-shafted Flicker
Horned Lark
Gray Jay
Steller's Jay
Scrub Jay
Pinyon Jay
Clark's Nutcracker

Black-billed Magpie
American Crow
Black-capped Chickadee
Mountain Chickadee
Plain Titmouse
American Dipper
Golden-crowned Kinglet
Mountain Bluebird
Townsend's Solitaire
Veery
Swainson's Thrush
Sage Thrasher
Western Tanager
Green-tailed Towhee
Chipping Sparrow
Gray-headed Junco
Brewer's Blackbird
Rosy Finch
Pine Grosbeak
Red Crossbill
Pine Siskin
Evening Grosbeak

Seasons

What "season" you are in depends upon where in Arizona you are located. Even such similar areas as Phoenix and Tucson can differ significantly. Although you can always expect temperatures over 100 degrees Fahrenheit by early to mid-April in Phoenix, the thermometers in Tucson generally don't hit the century mark until a month later.

Using the benchmark of 3 to 4 degrees per 1,000 feet of elevation gain, that means that the high plateaus of the northeastern part of the state would still be in the 60s and 70s as Phoenix swelters.

While southern Arizona is noted for its warm winters and searingly hot summers, the higher elevations of the Central Mountains, Colorado Plateau, and the Sky Islands have cold winters and mild summers.

Spring and fall are the premier times for birding in Arizona, but summers can be productive at the higher elevations. Winters are good along the Colorado River and in southwestern Arizona.

Migrations

Birds regularly move from breeding to winter ranges. No one completely knows why birds make their yearly migrations, but undoubtedly both food and weather affect when and where birds migrate.

Almost 100 of the 480 species of birds found in Arizona migrate long distances, either south from summer breeding grounds in the far north to winter in Arizona, or north from wintering grounds in Mexico and Central and South America to breed and raise their young in Arizona. Many others migrate shorter distances within the state, primarily from one elevation to another.

Spring migrations are direct, tightly packed moves with one common goal, to get to the summer breeding grounds.

Fall migrations are more widespread and loose as the flocks head for winter feeding grounds. The natural drive is very different, and there is not the hurry in the fall migration found in the spring. Fall movement is much more dependent upon the weather and food supply, for the urgency to breed is not the driving force.

The altitude migrations are even less time-driven. These are made purely according to weather and food supply, and may take place at widely varying times each year.

Migration routes in Arizona follow a north-south pattern, and two major corridors carry most of the migrants. The wetlands and lakes of the Colorado River are major wintering grounds for large numbers of waterfowl and wading birds. As fall comes these geese, ducks, and wading birds begin to straggle into areas such as the Imperial National Wildlife Refuge, where they will stay until the breeding urge pushes them north in early spring.

On the other side of the state smaller birds, mostly passerines, move north and south during the same periods. This is when you can see Mexican Chickadee, Rosy Finch, Elegant Trogon, and dozens of other rare and wonderful birds with relative ease.

Map legend

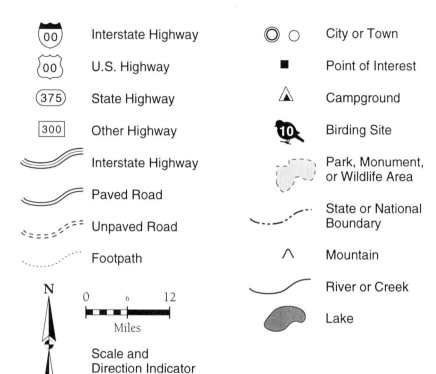

(00)	Interstate Highway	◎ ○	City or Town
(00)	U.S. Highway	■	Point of Interest
(375)	State Highway	▲	Campground
300	Other Highway	🐦10	Birding Site
≈	Interstate Highway		Park, Monument, or Wildlife Area
	Paved Road		State or National Boundary
= = =	Unpaved Road		
····	Footpath	∧	Mountain
			River or Creek
N 0 6 12 Miles	Scale and Direction Indicator		Lake

CHAPTER 3

Arizona's best birding areas

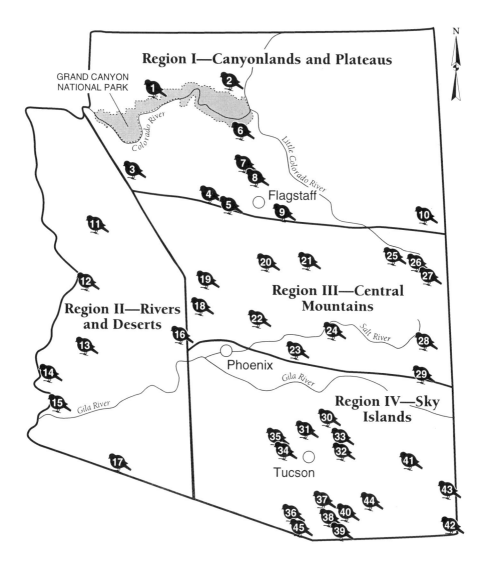

Prairie Falcons can be seen in many areas of this wild, vast region where many cliffs provide excellent nesting and roosting sites.

Northern Arizona
Canyonlands and plateaus

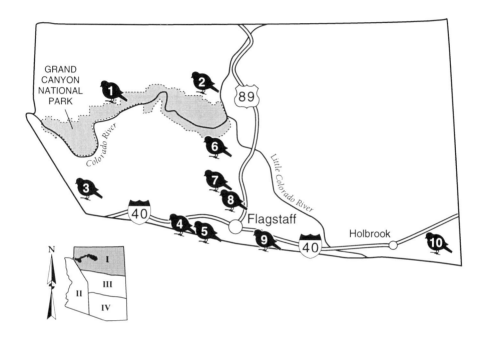

Pronghorns are not as plentiful in the state as they once were, but you can almost always see them along drives through open grasslands such as those on the way to Mount Trumbull.

1. Mount Trumbull area ————————————————

Habitats: Open grasslands, pinyon-juniper woodlands, ponderosa pine forest, and alpine.

Key birds: Chukar, Pinyon Jay, Northern Flicker, Great Horned Owl, Chipping Sparrow, Rosy Finch, Western Tanager, Ash-throated Flycatcher, White-breasted Nuthatch, and Wild Turkey.

Best times to bird: Spring and fall. Summer for birds at higher altitudes. The road to this region is generally impassable during winter and early spring.

General information

Of the three roads into the Mount Trumbull area, the one that heads south from Arizona Route 389 about 8 miles west of Fredonia is the best. The route is marked as the Mount Trumbull Recreation Area turnoff, and is considered an all-weather road. It can be muddy and slippery after heavy rains, though, and is frequently impassable during the winter months because of snow.

The route through the recreation area is 50 miles of dirt road from AZ 389, and there are no homes, ranches, or services along the way. Be prepared to handle any and all emergencies yourself, and carry adequate provisions. This is not a day trip. Plan on at least an overnight stay.

Mount Trumbull area

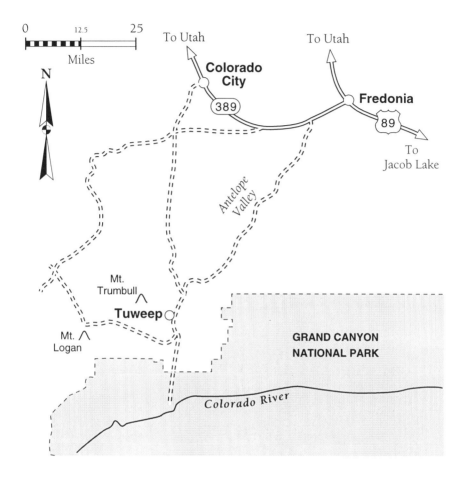

The first section of road crosses open grasslands where pronghorn antelope still roam, and gradually climbs into a pinyon-juniper zone near the base of the mountain.

Pinyon-juniper woodlands broken by occasional growths of manzanita and shrub live-oak cover the lower south slopes of the peak. An unbroken ponderosa pine forest covers the northern slopes and higher elevations all around the mountain.

Birding information

The grasslands along the first section of the road are one of the few areas in Arizona to see Chukar, and with increasing proximity to the mountain Pinyon Jays may be visible.

At Nixon Springs Wild Turkey are evident in the spring as they strut, and in the fall. Steller's Jay, Northern Flicker, Ash-throated Flycatcher, Western Bluebird, and Chipping Sparrow may be encountered by those who climb up the slope. Higher up, raptors such as Prairie Falcon, Red-tailed Hawk, and Golden Eagle are frequently seen.

Extremely lucky birders may spot Rosy Finch at the higher elevations around snowfields.

Additional help

Elevation: Peak is 8,028 feet and surrounding plateau is between 5,000 and 6,000 feet.

Hazards: Isolation. Few people explore this region, and it can be a while before help arrives. Several large ranches exist along the road on the plateau, but they are quite a distance from the road and Mount Trumbull.

Recreational Map of Arizona location: A3, A4, B3, B4

Nearest food, gas, and lodging: Sixty miles away in Fredonia.

Camping: On BLM lands, or at a primitive campground at Nixon Springs, where there is water.

Land ownership and/or contact: Bureau of Land Management, Vermillion Resource Area.

2. North Rim and Kaibab Plateau Parkway ————

Habitats: Ponderosa pine forest, mountain meadows, and spruce-fir forest at higher elevations.

Key birds: Blue Grouse, Red Crossbill, Williamson's Sapsucker, Clark's Nutcracker, and Goshawks.

Best times to bird: After snow melts in spring and before it falls in autumn.

General information:

This route is closed from November 15th to May 15th each year because of heavy snow, and in years of especially heavy snow it may be impossible to venture off the highway onto the forest roads until well into June or July.

North Rim Parkway (Arizona Route 67) is the only road into the North Rim of the Grand Canyon, and during midsummer is quite busy. This makes birding from the road difficult, and the best way to avoid the traffic is to wander along the many forest roads that lead west of the highway. These are maintained, and even low-clearance passenger vehicles can travel them safely. Several of them even lead into the park and to vista points above the canyon that are as spectacular as those at the more crowded North Rim at the end of the parkway. Contact the Forest Service for a map of the region that includes detailed information on all the forest roads.

In addition to birds, you can see large mule deer and Kaibab squirrel in the forest. The black-bellied, tassel-eared Kaibab squirrel is only found here and at Mount Trumbull.

Birding information:

This is an active birding area, and varied habitats of ponderosa pine forest, aspen groves, mountain meadows, and spruce-fir forests offer opportunities to view such species as Northern Goshawk, Wild Turkey, Blue Grouse, Williamson's Sapsucker, Clark's Nutcracker, Steller's Jay, Red Crossbill, Grace's Warbler, and a variety of woodpecker.

The best birding is off the highway and along the forest roads where few people venture. The best of these are Forest Roads 212, 230, and 429. All of

North Rim and Kaibab Plateau Parkway

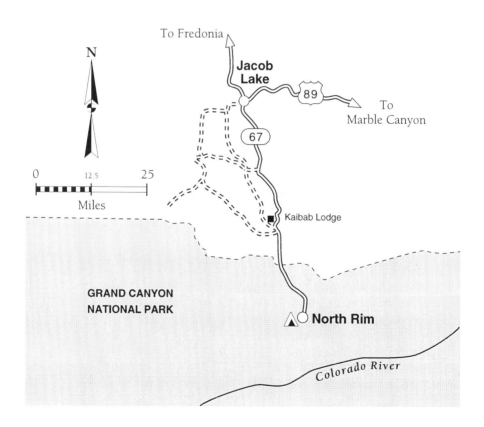

these head west from the highway and lead through all the habitat representative of the area.

Additional help:

Elevation: Between 8,000 and 9,000 feet.

Hazards: Early or late snow.

Recreational Map of Arizona location: A5, B5

Nearest food, gas, and lodging: Jacob Lake at junction of U.S. Highway 89 and North Rim Parkway, De Motte Park about 4 miles from Grand Canyon Village, and Grand Canyon Village along North Rim of canyon.

Camping: On national forest lands, at Forest Service campgrounds along parkway, and at national park campground along North Rim.

Land ownership and/or contact: Kaibab National Forest, North Kaibab Ranger District.

3. Aubrey Valley

Habitats: High cliffs, open grasslands, and pinyon-juniper woodlands. Prairie dog towns in grasslands.

Key birds: Prairie Falcon, Golden Eagle, Ferruginous Hawk, and Pinyon Jay.

Best times to bird: Nesting season in spring and soon after.

General information:

One option is to drive this area searching for raptors along a portion of historic Route (Arizona Route) 66. Another is to head into the backcountry to make a loop on improved dirt roads. For this loop, take the road to Rose Well north from Seligman up Chino Wash for about 20 miles. There, take a sharp turn back southwest along the top of a mesa as it winds down into Aubrey Valley to the west of the Aubrey Cliffs and back to Route 66 just east of the Grand Canyon Caverns.

The best birding locations are between the top of the mesa and Route 66. Since most birds are seen in the Aubrey Valley region just below the Aubrey Cliffs, it may be preferable to take the drive along Route 66 from Seligman to just before the Grand Canyon Caverns, then head northeast across Aubrey Valley on the road to Rose Well.

This is an easier drive, and it is possible to turn back to Route 66 before climbing to the top of the mesa.

Remember that most of this land is privately owned, and all birding should be done from the road.

Aubrey Valley

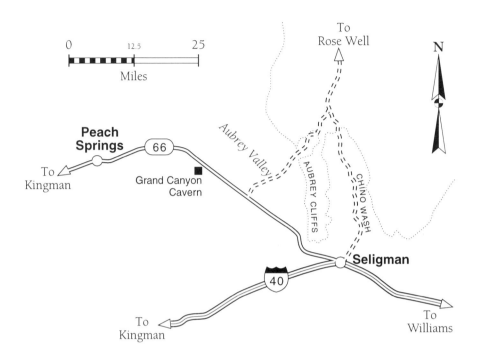

Birding information:

This is raptor country, and Golden Eagle are about as common along the route as Common Raven and Turkey Vulture. Large prairie dog towns along both Route 66 and the dirt roads to Rose Well provide great prey for the larger raptors and they frequently soar overhead. Keep an eye out for the towns as you drive along and then pull over to the side of the road and look skyward for soaring birds.

Additional help:

Elevation: About 6,000 feet.

Hazards: Few.

Recreational Map of Arizona location: C3, C4, D3, D4

Nearest food, gas, and lodging: Seligman to the east, Grand Canyon Caverns just to the west, and Peach Springs farther west.

Camping: None close by, except private campground at Grand Canyon Caverns.

Land ownership and/or contact: Mostly privately held land.

Coleman Lake;
White Horse Lake and Pine Flat route

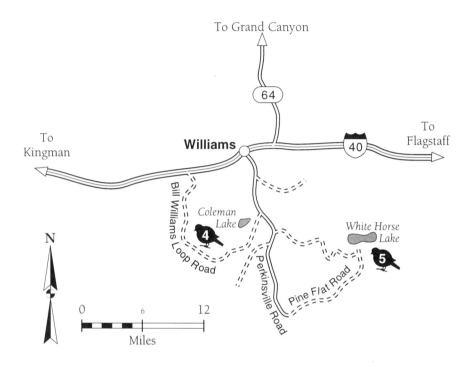

4. Coleman Lake

Habitats: Lake, wetlands, and ponderosa pine forest.

Key birds: Waterfowl (mostly ducks), Killdeer, Belted Kingfisher, Bald Eagle, and Wild Turkey.

Best times to bird: Late spring during breeding season. The road is generally closed from midwinter to early spring, which is when Bald Eagles winter. Try to see them in late December before the road is closed.

General information:

Coleman Lake has been improved as a wildlife habitat, and now there are islands and additional wetlands where birds thrive year-round.

The lake is only about 10 miles from Williams. To reach the lake, take Perkinsville Road (Forest Road 173) south for 7.5 miles and Forest Road 108 west for 2 miles. Though not very hard to reach, the area around the lake is lightly used much of the year and wildlife is abundant around it.

Heavy snowfall most winters causes the road to the lake to be frequently closed from January through March. If it is open during these times, be aware of any impending snowstorms in order to avoid getting snowed in.

Fall is a great time to visit. There are plenty of birds and other wildlife to see and some of the best fall color in Arizona.

Birding information:

While most birders come here for the water birds, there are also plenty of songbirds found in the surrounding ponderosa pine forest. These include jays, woodpeckers, warblers, and other passerines that breed and migrate through the region. Wild Turkey are also present in the forest at the edge of the meadow.

Water birds such as Belted Kingfisher, several species of ducks, Osprey, and Bald Eagle attract the most attention here, though, and they are found in large numbers from spring breeding season through the fall migration. Bald Eagle winter at the lake, and you can generally see a number of them before the road closes for the winter.

Walking around the perimeter of the lake is easy, and sightings of the above-mentioned birds are frequent.

Additional help:

Elevation: About 7,000 feet.

Hazards: Early or late snow.

Recreational Map of Arizona location: C4

Nearest food, gas, and lodging: Williams, about 10 miles north.

Camping: On national forest lands or in developed Forest Service campgrounds at Dogtown Reservoir and White Horse Lake about 10 miles to the east.

Land ownership and/or contact: Kaibab National Forest, Williams Ranger District.

5.   White Horse Lake and Pine Flat route ——————

Habitats: Ponderosa pine forest, pinyon-juniper and oak woodlands, open grasslands, and wetlands around lakes.

Key birds: Osprey, Bald Eagle, Steller's Jay, Clark's Nutcracker, Wild Turkey, Gambel's Quail, Acorn Woodpecker, Northern Pygmy-Owl, Spotted Owl, various species of waterfowl, Belted Kingfisher, Killdeer, and Lewis' Woodpecker.

Best times to bird: Spring for breeding season, and winter for Bald Eagle.

General information:

This trip is a 50-mile loop, and easily done in a day. The forest roads lead through stands of ponderosa pine, oak woodlands, and open grasslands on the way to White Horse Lake along Perkinsville and White Horse Lake roads.

White Horse Lake is a heavily used recreation area with full facilities, and birding around the lake is often hampered by the heavy use.

For a closer view of birds, head for lightly used J. D. Lake nearby where only a few fly fishermen congregate. All of the birds seen at White Horse Lake are also seen at J. D. Lake, but the crowds are not there to interfere with your birding.

The loop continues past the lakes and through more ponderosa pine forest, oak woodlands, and open grasslands as you return to Perkinsville Road, along which you return to Williams.

Birding information:

Birders come to the area for the many water-associated birds, such as Belted Kingfisher, Osprey, various ducks and cormorants, and Bald Eagle, found at the lakes. Most can be viewed from a distance, and the crowds don't bother viewers. Steller's Jay and Clark's Nutcracker congregate at places heavily used by people and are found in large numbers around the lakes.

For the more people-shy birds, such as Wild Turkey and passerines that are found in the nearby forests, you will want to wander away from the lakes, particularly White Horse. Fortunately, this is quite easy, because few people stop along the roads or venture into the forests.

Spotted Owl and Northern Pygmy Owl reside in the forests, along with Acorn and Lewis' Woodpeckers. Gamble's Quail can be seen all along the route.

Additional help:

Elevation: About 7,000 feet.

Hazards: Early or late snow.

Recreational Map of Arizona location: D5

Nearest food, gas, and lodging: Williams, about 15 miles to the north.

Camping: At Forest Service campground at lake.

Land ownership and/or contact: Kaibab National Forest, Williams Ranger District.

Gambel's Quail are found throughout Arizona, and they are especially abundant on the northern plateaus.

6. Grandview Point and Forest Road 302 loop ———

Habitats: Ponderosa pine forest and pinyon-juniper woodlands.

Key birds: Hairy Woodpecker, Northern Flicker, Western Flycatcher, Mountain Chickadee, Pygmy Nuthatch, Pinyon Jay, Northern Saw-whet Owl, and Three-toed Woodpecker.

Best times to bird: Spring breeding season.

General information:

This route leads you into the forests along the South Rim of the Grand Canyon, away from the crowds that cause bumper-to-bumper traffic jams near the canyon. Forest Road 302 wanders through ponderosa and pinyon-juniper forests from Tusayan to Grandview Point on the South Rim, and from there it is possible to return to Arizona Route 64 about 12 miles south of Tusayan

Grandview Point and Forest Road 302 loop

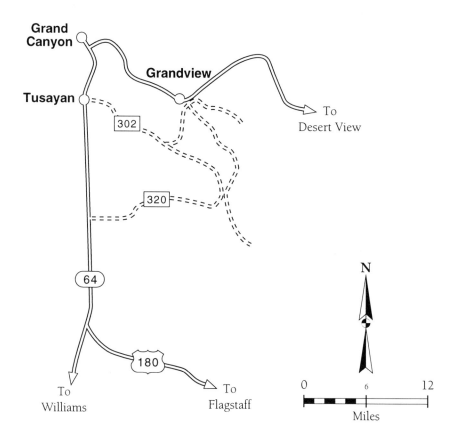

via Forest Roads 310, 311, and 320 or to Tusayan along Forest Roads 301 and 302.

There are no facilities along this 45-mile-long route, and heavy traffic along the roads is generally limited to big-game hunting season in the fall.

Although these roads can be traveled in even low-clearance vehicles they do get muddy and slippery after heavy rains or after the snow melts in late spring. Winter snow closes the roads.

Birding information:

Birding here is primarily for songbirds. Three-toed and Hairy Woodpecker, Northern Saw-whet Owl, Pygmy Nuthatch, Mountain Chickadee, Northern Flicker, Gambel's Quail, and Western Flycatcher are all abundant here, and Wild Turkey can be seen during spring strut.

Keep an eye out above for soaring raptors such as Red-tailed Hawk and Golden Eagle. Prairie Falcon are also spotted.

Additional help:

Elevation: About 7,000 feet.

Hazards: Dirt roads, isolation, and early or late snow.

Recreational Map of Arizona location: C5

Nearest food, gas, and lodging: Tusayan, where the route begins.

Camping: On national forest lands. No developed campgrounds outside park.

Land ownership and/or contact: Kaibab National Forest, Tusayan Ranger District.

7. Red Butte and Red Mountain loop

Habitats: Volcanic buttes, steep cliffs, pinyon-juniper woodlands.

Key birds: Golden Eagle, Prairie Falcon, Red-tailed Hawk, Common Raven, Pinyon Jay, Gambel's Quail.

Best times to bird: Breeding season in late spring.

General information:

Both Red Butte and Red Mountain are volcanic formations that rise above surrounding pinyon-juniper forests and provide excellent nesting sites for various raptors.

A road encircles Red Butte and a mile-long trail leads to the top. This is an excellent place to watch for wildlife and view the flatlands all the way to the Grand Canyon. Don't attempt to climb on the bluffs, for it is both dangerous to the climber and disturbs nesting birds. Climbing Red Mountain is prohibited by law, and anyone who disturbs nesting raptors there is liable for arrest. A mile-long trail does lead from a parking area to the base of the cliffs, and you can scan the cliff face for nests.

The parking area for Red Mountain is located about 0.5 mile off US Highway 180, 31 miles north of Flagstaff. To reach the parking area for Red Butte, head north on Arizona Route 64 from its junction with US 180 for about 11 miles to Forest Road 320. Head east for 1 mile to Forest Road 340, and turn north for just under 1 mile to Forest Road 340A. Head east for less than 0.5 mile to the parking area and trailhead.

Birding information:

This is a great place to view raptors. The bluffs and cliffs of the two volcanic formations offer exceptional nesting and roosting sites for Golden Eagle, Prairie Falcon, Red-tailed Hawk, and Common Raven. During nesting times you should be able to spot plenty of these species as they search for prey and return to the nests to feed their young.

Red Butte and Red Mountain loop;
Lamar Haines Memorial Wildlife Area

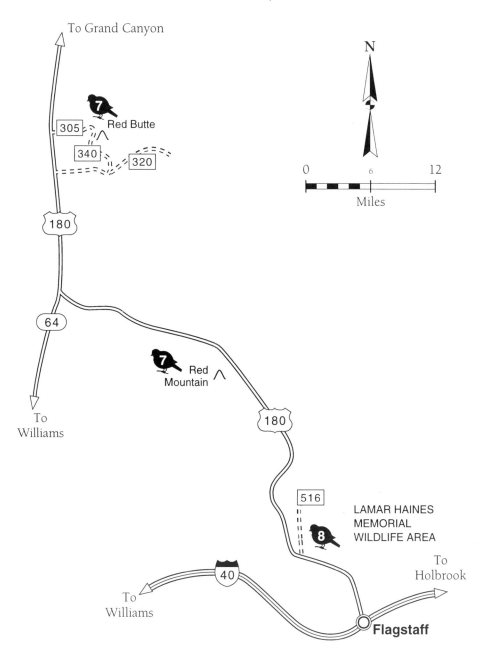

Additional help:

> **Elevation:** About 6,500 to 7,000 feet.
>
> **Hazards:** Rough roads.
>
> **Recreational Map of Arizona location:** C5
>
> **Nearest food, gas, and lodging:** Tusayan, Valle, Williams, and Flagstaff.
>
> **Camping:** On national forest lands. No nearby developed campgrounds.
>
> **Land ownership and/or contact:** Kaibab National Forest, Tusayan Ranger District, and Coconino National Forest, Peaks Ranger District.

8. Lamar Haines Memorial Wildlife Area

> **Habitats:** Ponderosa forest, mountain meadows, fir-aspen forest, and wetlands around creek and pond.
>
> **Key birds:** American Dipper, Lewis', Downy, Hairy, and Three-toed Woodpeckers, Red-breasted and White-breasted Nuthatches, Brown Creeper, and Mountain Chickadee.
>
> **Best times to bird:** Spring through fall.

General information:

This wildlife area is located on an old homestead at the base of the San Francisco Peaks. Large ponderosa pine grow in the area, and mixed aspen-fir forests surround several meadows. Mountain meadows are fed by springs, and a small creek and pond are fed by the spring waters.

The area is off U.S. Highway 180 on Snowbowl Road (Forest Road 516) about 7 miles northwest of Flagstaff. Follow the signs to the wildlife area 4.5 miles off US 180.

Several trails lead from the parking area to the old homestead site and into the surrounding national forest.

Birding information:

Songbirds that inhabit mixed conifer forests are abundant here. Look for Lewis', Downy, Hairy, and Three-toed Woodpeckers, Mountain Chickadee, Western Flycatcher, Red-breasted and White-breasted Nuthatches, and Brown Creeper.

Watch closely for cavity-nesting birds as you hike along the trails to the meadows.

Mourning Doves are found in mixed forests and open areas.

Additional help:

Elevation: About 8,000 feet.

Hazards: Few.

Recreational Map of Arizona location: D5

Nearest food, gas, and lodging: Flagstaff.

Camping: On national forest land. Nearest developed campgrounds are south of Flagstaff and at Sunset Crater to the northeast.

Land ownership and/or contact: Arizona Fish and Game Department, Region 2.

9. Mormon Lake area

Habitats: Large lake with mudflats, wetlands, open grasslands, cliffs, and mixed-conifer forest.

Key birds: Peregrine Falcon, Prairie Falcon, Osprey, Bald Eagle, Cliff Swallow, Horned Lark, Eared Grebe, Redhead, Common and Lesser Nighthawks, Band-tailed Pigeon, Flammulated and Saw-whet Owls, Gambel's Quail, and Steller's Jay.

Best times to bird: In Spring, from March through April and in fall, from September through November.

General information:

This is the largest lake in Arizona, covering more than 2,000 acres, but it is only 6 feet deep at its deepest spot. During dry years it sometimes dries up completely, but it generally covers at least 500 acres.

Paved Lake Mary Road leads from Flagstaff to Mormon Lake, and paved Forest Road 90 encircles the lake.

Although fishing is poor and the lake is too shallow for boating, Mormon Lake is a popular getaway for Flagstaff residents. This has led to considerable

Mormon Lake area

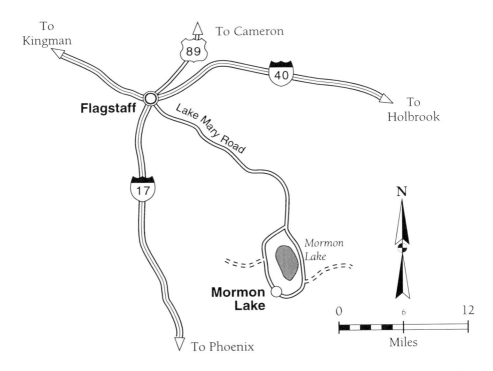

Open grasslands with mountains in the distance become radiant as the sun breaks through the clouds of an afternoon thunderstorm.

development, and there are two campgrounds in addition to private in-holdings nearby.

The lake lies at 7,300 feet, and a mix of habitat is found there. Open water and wetlands give way to open grasslands. These in turn are surrounded by conifer forests. Cliffs rise above the lake on the east side.

Birding information:

Osprey and Peregrine Falcon can be seen here year round, and Bald Eagle winter over. Just about every species of waterfowl seen in Arizona comes through the area between March and April and September through November.

The cliffs are home to Rock Wren and falcons, and other raptors who use them as nesting and roosting sites. Saw-whet, Spotted, and Screech Owls are heard in the adjoining forest.

Gambel's Quail and Horned Lark are found in the grasslands.

Additional help:

Elevation: About 7,300 feet.

Hazards: Early or late snow.

Recreational Map of Arizona location: D6

Nearest food, gas, and lodging: Flagstaff.

Camping: At developed Forest Service campgrounds at lake.

Land ownership and/or contact: Coconino National Forest, Mormon Lake Ranger District.

10. Petrified Forest drive

Habitats: High desert open grasslands and badlands.

Key birds: Ferruginous Hawk, Prairie Falcon, Golden Eagle, Scaled Quail, Greater Roadrunner, Western Wood-Pewee, Horned Lark, Cliff Swallow, Bendire's Thrasher, Sage Thrasher, Western Tanager, Chipping Sparrow.

Best times to bird: Spring through fall, with the best birding during breeding season.

General information:

The drive through the Painted Desert and Petrified Forest National Park, which is off Interstate 40 about 25 miles east of Holbrook, leads through some

---

Petrified Forest drive

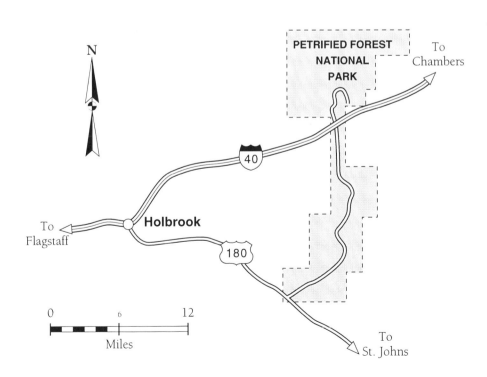

of the most haunting landscapes in the state. Few plants grow in these badlands, and visitors primarily come to see the scenic hills and petrified trees rather than the flora and fauna.

Summer can be hot here, and winter winds can chill you to the bone.

Birding information:

There are limited birds along this road, but those seen are representative of the high desert country of the Navajo Reservation and northeastern Arizona. Look for them at any stops along the road, and watch for raptors soaring overhead.

Additional help:

Elevation: About 5,500 feet.

Hazards: Occasional rattlesnakes, and lack of water in backcountry.

Recreational Map of Arizona location: D8

Nearest food, gas, and lodging: Holbrook to the west and Gallup to the east.

Camping: None except backcountry.

Land ownership and/or contact: Petrified Forest National Park.

Western Arizona
River and deserts

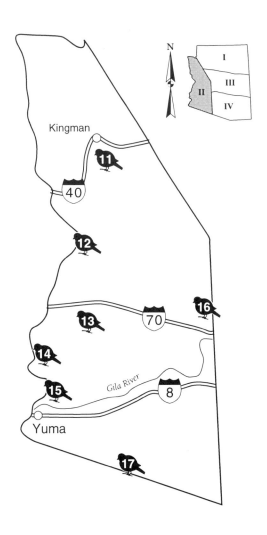

N

I

II

III

IV

Kingman

11

40

12

16

13

70

14

15

Gila River

8

Yuma

17

Elf and Screech Owls frequently inhabit the vacated homes of Gila Woodpecker and Gilded Flicker in tall saguaro.

11. Hualapai Mountain Park and Wabayuma Peak Wilderness

Habitats: Ponderosa pine forest and pinyon-juniper woodlands.

Key birds: Flammulated, Great Horned, and Spotted Owls; Western Screech Owl; Ladder-backed and Hairy Woodpeckers; Prairie Falcon, Golden Eagle, and Ferruginous Hawk.

Best times to bird: Spring breeding season.

General information:

It takes less than 30 minutes to drive from high desert with Joshua trees to ponderosa pine-covered peaks in this county park near Kingman. The elevation at Kingman is 3,340 feet, and at the entrance to the park is 4,984 feet. The highest point in the park is 8,417 feet. This is in the Canadian Life Zone, and birdlife here is dramatically different from that found lower.

Both Hualapai Mountain Park and Wabayuma Peak Wilderness Area are lightly used except in midsummer, and even then it is easy to get away from crowds while birding.

Birding information:

At the lower elevations expect to see birds typical of high desert such as Gambel's Quail, Greater Roadrunner, Curve-billed Thrasher, Hooded and Scott's Orioles, and White-winged Dove. As you climb higher into the

Hualapai Mountain Park and Wabayuma Peak Wilderness

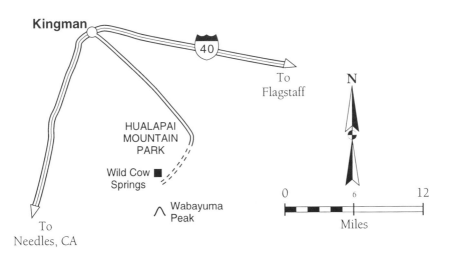

White-winged Doves feed upon the nectar and seeds of saguaro blooms.

ponderosa pine forest you can see Ladder-backed and Hairy Woodpeckers, along with other songbirds common to the pine forest. Raptors such as Golden Eagle, Prairie Falcon, and Ferruginous Hawk soar overhead, and you can find Flammulated, Great Horned, and Spotted Owls and Western Screech-Owl in the deep forest.

While birding is easiest in the developed areas of the county park, there is less human disturbance in the area around Wild Cow Campground and Wabayuma Peak.

Additional help:

Elevation: Between 5,000 and 8,500 feet.

Hazards: Rough roads from park to boundary of the wilderness area.

Recreational Map of Arizona location: D2

Nearest food, gas, and lodging: Kingman.

Camping: In county park and on BLM land at Wild Cow Campground.

Land ownership and/or contact: Hualapai Mountain Park and Bureau of Land Management, Kingman Resource Area.

12. Bill Williams Delta National Wildlife Refuge, Bill Williams Gorge, and Alamo Lake State Park

Habitats: Wetlands, open water, river bottomlands with willow-cottonwood forest, rocky desert, and saguaro stands.

Key birds: Snow and Canada Geese, Clark's Grebe, various species of egret, Double-crested Cormorant, White Pelican, Ash-throated Flycatcher, White-winged and Inca Doves, Sharp-shinned Hawk, Lesser Nighthawk, Gila and Ladder-backed Woodpeckers, Verdin, Phainopepla, Yellow-headed Blackbird, six species of warblers, and Blue Grosbeak.

Best times to bird: Spring breeding season and November through January for migrants.

Bill Williams Delta National Wildlife Refuge, Bill Williams Gorge, and Alamo Lake State Park

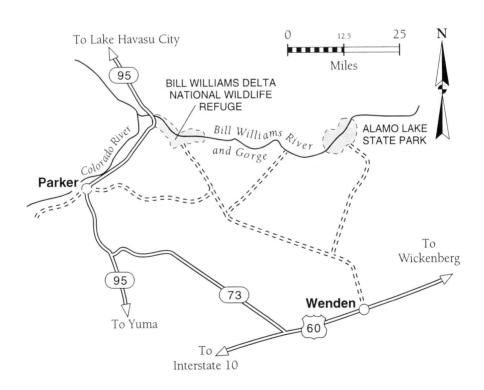

Curve-billed Thrashers do not seem to fear the spines of cactus.

General information:

This birding area extends from the banks of Lake Havasu near Parker Dam up the Bill Williams River to Alamo Lake State Park. The habitats here change from open water and wetlands in the wildlife refuge through a beautiful river gorge to the large reservoir at Alamo Lake.

This trek includes a variety of habitats, but away from the water is raw desert.

Birding information:

The easiest birding is done in the wildlife refuge, where there are waterfowl galore plus upland birds such as Gambel's Quail, Curve-billed Thrasher, White-winged and Inca Doves, Phainopepla, Blue Grosbeak, and six types of warblers.

In the river gorge you are most likely to sight Lesser Nighthawk, Verdin, Gila and Ladder-backed Woodpeckers, Ash-throated Flycatcher, and Sharp-shinned Hawk.

Plenty of waterfowl frequent Alamo Lake, and desert birds inhabit the gorge and refuge uplands.

Additional help:

Elevation: About 2,000 feet.

Hazards: Summer heat and some rattlesnakes.

Recreational Map of Arizona location: E2, E3

Nearest food, gas, and lodging: Lake Havasu City and Parker.

Camping: At Lakes Havasu and Alamo state parks, Buckskin State Park, and county parks near Cross Roads. Also primitive camping on BLM lands.

Land ownership and/or contact: Alamo Lake State Park, Bureau of Land Management, Phoenix District Office, Bureau of Land Management, Havasu Resource Area, and Bill Williams Delta National Wildlife Refuge.

13. Kofa National Wildlife Refuge

Habitats: Desert canyon and creosote-covered flatlands.

Key birds: Greater Roadrunner, Canyon Wren, Brown Towhee, Sage Thrasher, Hooded Oriole, Phainopepla, Golden Eagle, Cliff Swallow, White-winged Dove, and various gnatcatchers.

Best times to bird: Spring breeding season.

General information:

Kofa National Wildlife Refuge was established to protect the habitat of desert bighorn sheep, and its 1,000 square miles are an inhospitable place at best. It is a dangerous place with extremely high summer temperatures and lack of water.

Several roads cross the desert lands of the refuge from Arizona Route 95 to the higher peaks to the east but one should be careful about traveling along them.

Probably the most traveled and best maintained is the road into Palm Canyon off U.S. Highway 95 about 25 miles south of Quartzsite. This semi-oasis is also one of the best birding areas in the refuge.

Kofa National Wildlife Refuge

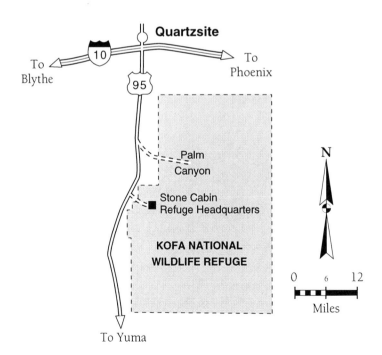

You may not find them being chased by wily coyotes, but you should find Greater Roadrunners throughout the southern part of Arizona.

Birding information:

From the parking area at the base of Palm Canyon a 0.5-mile-long trail leads you into the canyon where birding is decent year-round. Common avian inhabitants include Canyon Wren, Phainopepla, Hooded and Scott's Orioles, White-winged Dove, various gnatcatchers, Brown Towhee, Cliff Swallow, and Sage Thrasher. Overhead you may spot Golden Eagle, Red-tailed Hawk, and Prairie Falcon soaring on the thermals.

On the road into the canyon, Greater Roadrunner dart across the desert floor and thrashers and White-winged Dove fly from cactus to cactus.

Additional help:

Elevation: Between 500 and 5,000 feet.

Hazards: Isolation, desert heat, and lack of water.

Recreational Map of Arizona location: G2

Nearest food, gas, and lodging: Quartzsite to the north and Yuma to the south.

Camping: Primitive camping on the refuge.

Land ownership and/or contact: Kofa National Wildlife Refuge.

To an outsider, Palm Canyon in the Kofa National Wildlife Refuge
is a sparse and desolate place, but it is almost an oasis in the dry lands there.
Birding is good as you head up the canyon.

14. Imperial National Wildlife Refuge and Martinez Lake

Habitats: River marsh, open water, and open desert.

Key birds: Migrating waterfowl (Snow and Canada Geese, and a variety of ducks), White Pelican, Great Blue Heron, Snowy Egret, Sandhill Crane, Yuma Clapper Rail, Eared Grebe, Spotted, Least, and Western Sandpipers, Black Phoebe, Gambel's Quail, and Marsh Wren.

Best times to bird: Spring breeding season and fall migration. Migrants begin to settle in the area about November and stay until about the end of January.

General information:

Marshlands that extend for 30 miles along the Colorado River in this refuge are bordered by some of the hottest and driest desert lands in the nation. This contrast makes a visit to the refuge a rewarding one for birders, and most head for the refuge headquarters on the shore of Martinez Lake. Martinez Lake Road leads west off U.S. Highway 95 about 23 miles north of Yuma.

There you can pick up a checklist and information about the birds currently in residence at the refuge, as well as climb the viewing platform, which provides views of agricultural fields planted to feed waterfowl and expanses of marsh along the shore of Martinez Lake.

The observation tower at Martinez Lake in the Imperial National Wildlife Refuge rises from stark desert lands to look over the wide expanses of Martinez Lake along the Lower Colorado River.

Distant mountains tower above a flat desert wash covered with mesquite.

Several roads, particularly Red Cloud Mine Road, lead into good birding areas of the refuge highlands. About 3 miles from the refuge headquarters the 1-mile-long Painted Desert Trail offers a self-guiding tour of desert land, where birds are especially plentiful in winter.

Imperial National Wildlife Refuge and Martinez Lake; Mittry Lake and Betty's Kitchen

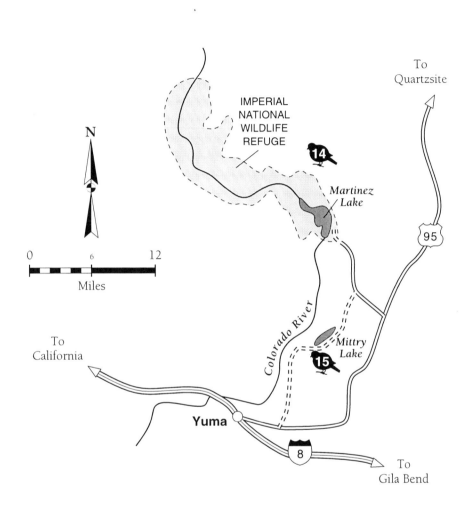

Birding information:

Migrating waterfowl winter over in the open water of the refuge, wading birds abound in the marshlands, songbirds thrive in the riparian growth along feeder streams and canals, and birds more normally associated with open desert are found in the refuge uplands.

Come here between November and January for the most prolific viewing times, and you can add a number of birds to your life list.

Additional help:

Elevation: About 500 feet.

Hazards: Summer heat, rattlesnakes, and lack of water in far reaches of refuge.

Recreational Map of Arizona location: G1, H1

Nearest food, gas, and lodging: Martinez Lake and Yuma.

Camping: Martinez Lake, and farther south at various lakes along the Colorado River.

Land ownership and/or contact: Imperial National Wildlife Refuge.

15. Mittry Lake and Betty's Kitchen

Habitats: Barren desert, wetlands, and marsh.

Key birds: Pied-billed Grebe, Great Blue Heron, various egrets, Yuma Clapper Rail, a variety of ducks, Phainopepla, Abert's Towhee, Green-backed Heron, Harris' Hawk, and Yellow-rumped and Orange-crowned Warblers.

Best times to bird: Spring breeding season and from November through January.

General information:

Mittry Lake is an oxbow lake in a bend of the Lower Colorado River above Laguna Dam about 10 miles north of Yuma. The Arizona Game and Fish Department has developed these wetlands and marshes as wildlife habitat.

Although many birds are visible from the shores of the wetlands, birders can see many more by canoeing around the edges of open waters as waterfowl congregate during the winter. If you choose not to canoe, there are other great views from the access road along the Gila Gravity Canal.

Just south of Mittry Lake at Betty's Kitchen the Bureau of Land Management has developed a self-guiding, 0.5-mile trail that winds through riparian vegetation along the Colorado River.

Birding information:

This is the best place in Arizona to see wintering waterfowl. In addition, the Yuma Clapper Rail, although not easily seen, is abundant in the marshes.

Additional help:

Elevation: About 500 feet.

Hazards: Rattlesnakes in desert.

Recreational Map of Arizona location: H1

Birding can be a lonely pursuit in the desert mountains of Arizona.

Nearest food, gas, and lodging: Yuma.

Camping: To the north along the Colorado River are several private campgrounds.

Land ownership and/or contact: Bureau of Land Management, Yuma Resource Area, and Arizona Game and Fish, Region IV.

16. Hassayampa River Preserve and Burro Creek ——

Habitats: Desert canyon and riparian woodlands.

Key birds: Great Blue Heron; Green-winged Teal; Sharp-shinned, Zone-tailed, and Harris' Hawks; Common Black Hawk; Mississippi Kite; American Dipper; Scrub Jay; Black-crowned Night Heron; Gambel's Quail; Inca Dove; Western Screech-Owl; Anna's Hummingbird; Ladder-backed Woodpecker; Cactus Wren; Verdin; Western Wood-Pewee; Hooded Oriole; Vermilion Flycatcher; and Crissal Thrasher.

Best times to bird: Spring breeding season and fall migration.

General information:

Both of these sites, along U.S. Highway 93 between Phoenix and Kingman, offer good birding in riparian woodlands unusual in this portion of Arizona.

The Nature Conservancy operates the Hassayampa River Preserve, which is located 3 miles southeast of Wickenburg to the west of US 93

Hassayampa River Preserve and Burro Creek

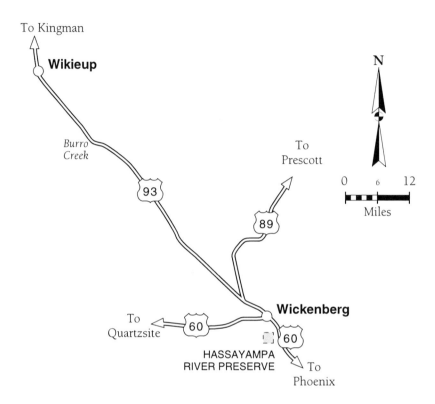

(also U.S. Highways 60 and 89 along this section). Exploration of the preserve is limited to the maintained and well-marked trails, but birding is excellent since these take you through lush riparian growth and around Palm Lake, where waterfowl congregate.

The Bureau of Land Management administers Burro Creek, which straddles US 93 about 40 miles northwest of Wickenburg and 11 miles southeast of Wikieup. Although the riparian growth is not as lush here as at Hassayampa Preserve there are fewer restrictions on your explorations.

Both sites include areas with open water and creekside vegetation, but Burro Creek also has creekside cliffs where swallows, swifts, and other cliff dwellers are abundant.

In addition, these areas are high enough in elevation that summer visits are not out of the question, although midday temperatures can reach 100 degrees.

Cactus Wrens nest among the sharp spines of the cholla where predators fear to tread.

Birding information:

Hassayampa River Preserve has well-marked, self-guiding trails that lead through a riparian habitat where 229 species of birds have been reported. These include Gray, Zone-tailed, and Sharp-shinned Hawks, and Mississippi Kite. The number of bird species reported at Burro Creek is somewhat less at about 190, but there is more freedom of movement here for those searching for elusive species.

Common Ground Doves can be seen in areas such as Organ Pipe Cactus National Monument.

Additional help:

Elevation: 2,500 to 3,000 feet.

Hazards: Few.

Recreational Map of Arizona location: Hassayampa River Preserve, F4; Burro Creek, E3

Nearest food, gas, and lodging: Wickenburg and Wikieup.

Camping: At BLM Campground at Burro Creek.

Land ownership and/or contact: The Hassayampa River Preserve, and Bureau of Land Management, Kingman Resource Area.

17. Organ Pipe Cactus National Monument ————

Habitats: Open desert, desert canyon, and desert springs.

Key birds: Vermilion Flycatcher; Rock Wren; Cactus Wren; Canyon Wren; Pyrrhuloxia; Phainopepla; Lucy's Warbler; Black Vulture; Cooper's and Harris' Hawks; Greater Roadrunner; Elf Owl; Common Poorwill; Gilded Flicker; Cordilleran Flycatcher; Rough-winged Swallow; Verdin; Long-billed Marsh Wren; Green-tailed Towhee; Bronzed Cowbird; and Hooded Oriole.

Best times to bird: Any time but midsummer.

Organ pipe and saguaro cacti flourish in the Organ Pipe Cactus National Monument in southwestern Arizona.

Organ Pipe Cactus National Monument

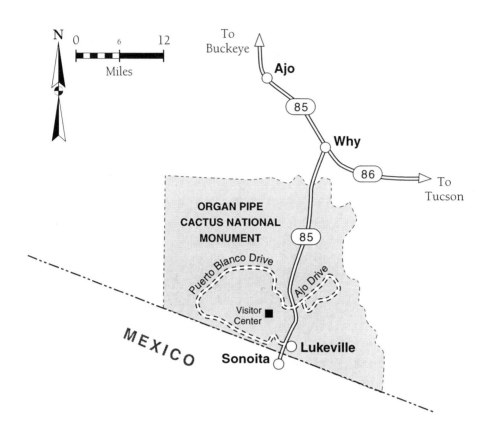

General information:

Organ Pipe Cactus National Monument includes over 330,000 acres of desert flatlands and mountains that lie just north of the Mexican border in some of the most desolate country in a state known for its desolate sites.

Most visitors congregate at the campground near the monument headquarters just north of the Mexican border, but the best birding is in the backcountry near the occasional oasis.

The most accessible of these is Quitobaquito Springs along Puerto Blanco Drive into the backcountry of the monument.

A shorter drive, but still one with plenty of birds, is the Ajo Mountain Drive that begins across Arizona Route 85 from the monument headquarters. This drive takes you up into Estes Canyon and to the trailhead to Bull Pasture.

Above:
The flora of desert mountains can be very diverse, as shown by this photo from the Ajo Mountains in Organ Pipe Cactus National Monument.

Left:
A permanent but rare resident of the southern deserts of Arizona is the Black Vulture.

Birding information:

The springs in the backcountry are magnets for many species of birds, some of which are migrants from Mexico, such as Cordilleran Flycatcher, seen in few other places in the United States. Even the drive into the Ajo Mountains leads to areas with a little more water, and birds congregate along the seasonal creeks where water is available late into the summer after wet winters.

Additional help:

Elevation: From 1,200 to 5,000 feet.

Hazards: Extreme summer heat, lack of water, rough roads, and rattlesnakes. As you enter the adjoining Cabeza Prieta National Wildlife Refuge, be aware that you are in a military bombing range.

Recreational Map of Arizona location: I3, I4

Nearest food, gas, and lodging: Lukeville, Why, and Ajo.

Camping: At a developed campground near monument headquarters, and primitive sites in backcountry.

Land ownership and/or contact: Organ Pipe Cactus National Monument.

Central Arizona
Mountains

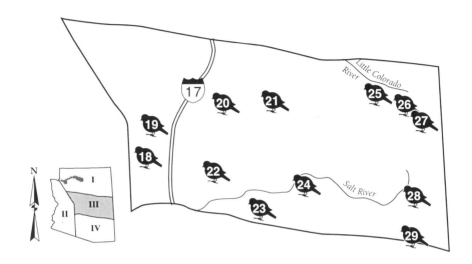

While Arizona's lower deserts are sparse country, many of the higher mountain ranges have plenty of vegetation covering them.

18. Dead Horse Ranch State Park and Tuvasci Marsh

Habitats: Open desert, oak woodlands, cottonwood/willow riparian woodlands, and marsh.

Key birds: Marsh Wren, Red-winged Blackbird, Gambel's Quail, Osprey, Bald Eagle, Great Blue Heron, Yellow-billed Cuckoo, Prairie Falcon, Belted Kingfisher, and a variety of waterfowl during migration time.

Best times to bird: Spring breeding season and from November through January.

General information:

This site is located on the Verde River just outside the town of Cottonwood at the southern end of Oak Creek Canyon. The park has full facilities for camping, and the marsh offers great wildlife viewing.

There is easy access to the park, and birders who like their creature comforts can find excellent food and lodging in nearby towns.

Birding information:

Birds of many types are drawn to the beaver ponds in Tuvasci Marsh, and the cottonwood-willow woodlands along the river attract still more. Trails

Dead Horse Ranch State Park and Tuvasci Marsh; Red Rock State Park

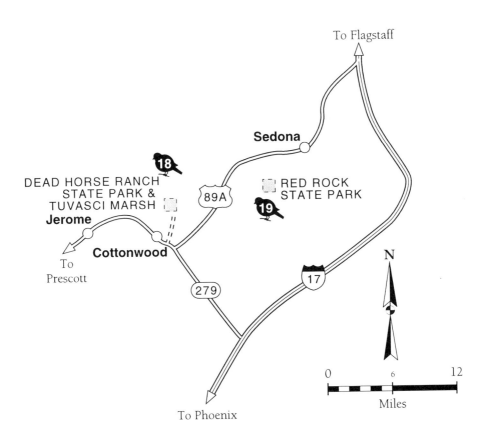

lead from the campground and park picnic area to both the marsh and the river, where there is good birding most of the year.

Additional help:

Elevation: About 4,000 feet.

Hazards: Few.

Recreational Map of Arizona location: E5

Nearest food, gas, and lodging: Cottonwood and Clarkdale.

Camping: At campground in park.

Land ownership and/or contact: Dead Horse Ranch State Park.

Arizona is home to many rare birds, but it also has its share of common ones such as this robin.

19. Red Rock State Park

Habitats: Riparian woodlands with willow, cottonwood, and sycamore.

Key birds: Bald Eagle; Common Black-Hawk; Vermilion Flycatcher; Western Tanager; Northern, Hooded, and Scott's Orioles; and half-a-dozen warblers.

Best times to bird: Spring breeding season and during fall migration.

General information:

Red Rock country surrounds this beautiful park setting. Large stands of cottonwood, willow, and sycamore provide homes for over 135 species of birds, and all the park development has been built to blend in with the surrounding environment. A well-marked trail system provides ready access to birding sites within the park, and plenty of other wildlife may be seen as well.

Birding information:

In the spring watch for nesting Common Black-Hawk. In the winter, search for Bald Eagle. Between spring and winter, both resident and migrant birds make this riparian area their home.

Additional help:

Elevation: About 4,500 feet.

Hazards: Few.

Recreational Map of Arizona location: E5

Nearest food, gas, and lodging: Sedona.

Camping: In park.

Land ownership and/or contact: Red Rock State Park.

20. Tonto Natural Bridge State Park ─────────

Habitats: Mountain canyon and riparian woodlands.

Key birds: American Dipper, Canyon Wren, Mountain Bluebird, Bell's Vireo, and Downy Woodpecker.

Best times to bird: Spring through fall.

General information:

This day outing 12 miles north of Payson on Arizona Route 87 includes the natural wonder of a travertine arch spanning 150 feet across Pine Canyon, 185 feet above the canyon floor. Spring water provides a lush habitat for wildlife, and a variety of birds congregate in the canyon. Explore the canyon along a trail that leads to the creek below, which is the best place to see birds.

Birding information:

Birding is good here year-round, but is especially good during the summer when migrants have reached the cool mountains as the desert below reaches over 100 degrees.

Additional help:

Elevation: About 5,000 feet.

Hazards: Few.

Recreational Map of Arizona location: E6

Nearest food, gas, and lodging: Payson and Pine.

Camping: At Forest Service campgrounds off Arizona Route 87 between Payson and the park.

Land ownership and/or contact: Tonto Natural Bridge State Park.

Tonto Natural Bridge State Park;
Canyon Creek and Tonto Creek Recreation Area

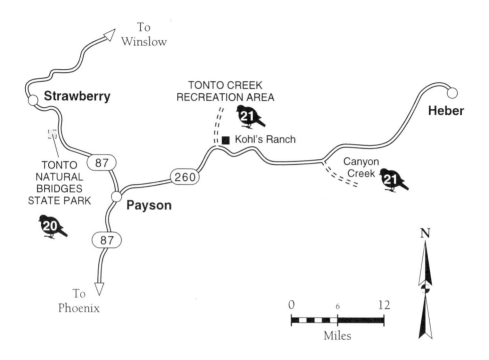

21. Canyon Creek and Tonto Creek Recreation Area

Habitats: Mountain meadows, ponderosa pine forest, and riparian woodlands.

Key birds: American Dipper, Acorn and Three-toed Woodpeckers, Western Bluebird, Red-naped Sapsucker, Black-chinned, Broad-tailed, and Rufous Hummingbirds, Yellow-rumped Warbler, and Wild Turkey.

Best times to bird: Spring through fall.

General information:

The Mogollon Rim cuts east-west across the middle of eastern Arizona. Several canyons just below this escarpment, which sharply divides the Mogollon Plateau from the desert 2,000 feet below, provide excellent birding sites.

Acorn Woodpeckers are abundant in the forests of the Central Mountains, as well as in the Sky Islands of the southeast.

The mixed oak-conifer forests here offer a variety of habitat for birds and other wildlife, and well-maintained forest roads lead into backcountry where few people venture.

Arizona Route 260 winds along below the rim for about 30 miles from Payson before it climbs to the top, and along that section the best birding occurs.

Birding information:

Spring and summer migrants utilize the wide variety of habitats and cool climate of this region, and songbirds of both conifer and oak forests abound here.

Additional help:

Elevation: About 5,000 feet.

Hazards: Rough roads.

Recreational Map of Arizona location: E6, E7

Nearest food, gas, and lodging: Payson, Kohl's Ranch, Forest Lakes, and Heber.

Camping: At Forest Service campgrounds along Arizona Route 260 above the Mogollon Rim.

Land ownership and/or contact: Tonto National Forest, Payson Ranger District.

22. Verde River and Horseshoe Dam

Habitats: Riparian woodlands surrounded by Sonoran Desert.

Key birds: Northern Cardinal, Vermilion Flycatcher, Northern (Bullock's) Oriole, Verdin, Bald Eagle, Harris' Hawk, Great Horned Owl, and Great Blue Heron.

Best times to bird: Spring breeding season and fall.

General information:

The Verde River cuts through vast expanses of Sonoran Desert, and the riparian growth along its banks provides food and nesting sites for birds year round. Horseshoe Reservoir is located on the Verde River about 50 miles north of Phoenix on Scottsdale or Cave Creek roads, and some 25 miles beyond Carefree, the last Phoenix-area settlement.

Birding information:

Look for birds that are attracted to the water. Northern Cardinal, Vermilion Flycatcher, Northern (Bullock's) Oriole, Verdin, and Black-tailed Gnatcatcher are some of the songbirds found here. Raptors commonly seen in the area include Harris' and Red-tailed Hawks and Bald Eagle.

This is one place to possibly find Great Horned Owl roosting in tall trees near the river and reservoir during the day.

Additional help:

Elevation: About 2,000 feet.

Hazards: High summer heat and lack of water.

Recreational Map of Arizona location: F5

Nearest food, gas, and lodging: Carefree.

Large owls, such as this Great Horned Owl, can be heard in the forests of the Central Mountains.

Camping: At campground near reservoir, and primitive camping on national forest land.

Land ownership and/or contact: Tonto National Forest, Cave Creek Ranger District.

Verde River and Horseshoe Dam

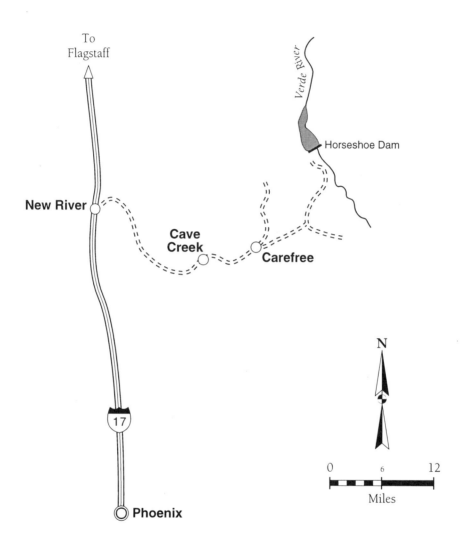

23. Phon D. Sutton Recreation Area

Habitats: Riparian woodlands surrounded by Sonoran Desert.

Key birds: Bald Eagle, Osprey, Harris' Hawk, Phainopepla, Gambel's Quail, Cactus Wren, and many warblers.

Best times to bird: Spring and fall.

General information:

This riparian habitat sits at the junction of the Verde and Salt rivers to the north of Mesa, and the flow of both of these is controlled upstream. This provides a steady flow of water into the recreation area that is unusual in the low desert. A nature trail passes through both the desert and riparian habitats found there.

Harris' Hawks are abundant in many areas of the state.

Phon D. Sutton Recreation Area;
Fish Creek and Roosevelt Lake Wildlife Area

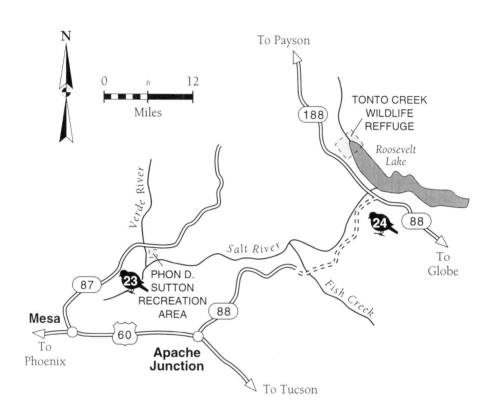

Birding information:

This is one of the few places in the Arizona deserts to find nesting Bald Eagle, and they are joined by Harris' and Red-tailed Hawks, and Osprey.

Desert species are found along the nature trail, and riparian species flock to the vegetation near the water.

Additional help:

Elevation: About 2,000 feet.

Hazards: High summer heat and lack of water.

Recreational Map of Arizona location: C5

Nearest food, gas, and lodging: Mesa.

Camping: Self-contained units at recreation site during winter, and at various campgrounds along the Salt River above the recreation site all year.

Land ownership and/or contact: Tonto National Forest, Mesa Ranger District.

24. Fish Creek and Roosevelt Lake Wildlife Area ⸺

Habitats: Riparian woodlands, open water, and shoreline.

Key birds: Osprey, Bald Eagle, Canada Goose, Gambel's Quail, Gila Woodpecker, Cactus Wren, Curve-billed Thrasher, Harris' and Red-tailed Hawks, and various ducks.

Best times to bird: Spring breeding and fall migration. Winter between November and January is best for geese and other waterfowl.

General information:

The Apache Trail (Arizona Route 88) winds through the Superstition Mountains as it follows the general path of the Salt River. Along the stretch of road between the towns of Apache Junction and Roosevelt, several large gorges of

The Northern Cardinal is regularly seen throughout much of Arizona.

Birds congregate along streams such as this one, since water is scarce in the desert and even much of the Central Mountains region.

tributaries cut through the desert mountains. Along the streams in the gorges, riparian growth provides excellent habitat for birds. One of these streams is Fish Creek, where willow, cottonwood, Arizona walnut, and ash trees provide luxurious (at least by Arizona desert standards) habitat.

Farther upstream on the Salt River stands Roosevelt Dam, one of the first water reclamation projects in Arizona and the West. The large reservoir behind the dam provides a ready source of water in the Sonoran Desert, and wintering waterfowl are attracted there in large numbers. The Tonto Creek arm of the lake is a wildlife refuge and some areas are closed to entry during the winter for the protection of the waterfowl.

Birding information:

The riparian woodlands in Fish Creek are home to songbirds such as Canyon Wren, Northern Cardinal, Pyrrhuloxia, Phainopepla, and Vermilion Flycatcher, which are all found in abundance.

Great Blue Heron, Black-crowned Night Heron, and Yellow-billed Cuckoo are just some of the birds that are found around Roosevelt Lake in addition to the wintering waterfowl. Bald Eagle also winter at the lake, and Osprey are found there year-round.

Additional help:

Elevation: Between 3,000 and 4,000 feet.

Hazards: High summer heat and rough roads.

Recreational Map of Arizona location: G6

Nearest food, gas, and lodging: Roosevelt, Apache Junction, and Tortilla Flat.

Camping: At campgrounds at Apache, Canyon, and Roosevelt lakes.

Land ownership and/or contact: Tonto National Forest, Tonto Basin Ranger District.

25. Allen Severson Wildlife Area and Jacques Marsh

Habitats: Artificial marshlands.

Key birds: Waterfowl such as Mallard, Northern Pintail, Redhead, Canvasback, Green-winged, Blue-winged, and Cinnamon Teals, Gadwall, Yellow-headed Blackbird, Great Blue Heron, Killdeer, and Belted Kingfisher.

Best times to bird: Spring breeding season and fall migration.

General information:

These two sites are artificial wetlands that were formed through the cooperation of the USDA Forest Service and several small communities in the White Mountains of north-central Arizona. Near the towns of Show Low and Pinetop, these marsh complexes were formed to treat wastewater effluent, and, as a byproduct, form wetlands that have become home to a large number of waterfowl that come there to breed and spend the summer. Some even winter over.

Killdeer are found in open fields near water throughout the northern portion of Arizona.

Birding information:

In addition to the waterfowl and wading birds that are attracted to these islands of marshland in the midst of grasslands and ponderosa pine forest, you can find Yellow-headed Blackbird, Belted Kingfisher, and Killdeer.

Additional help:

Elevation: About 6,500 feet.

Hazards: Few.

Recreational Map of Arizona location: F8

Nearest food, gas, and lodging: Show Low and Pinetop-Lakeside.

Camping: At Forest Service campgrounds between Show Low and Pinetop.

Land ownership and/or contact: Apache-Sitgreaves National Forest, Lakeside Ranger District.

Allen Severson Wildlife Area and Jacques Marsh

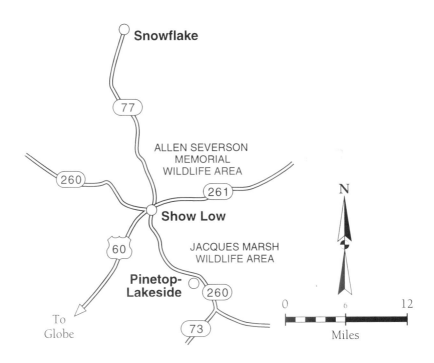

26. Springerville and Big Lake loop

Habitats: Mountain meadows, ponderosa pine forest, marsh, and riparian woodlands.

Key birds: Western Bluebird, Horned Lark, Great Blue Heron, Red-winged and Yellow-headed Blackbirds, Canada Goose, and Belted Kingfisher.

Best times to bird: Spring breeding season and fall migration.

General information:

A wide variety of mountain habitat is located along this route in the White Mountains. Large stands of ponderosa pine forest, open mountain meadows, riparian habitat along mountain streams, mountain lakes, and two of the best high-mountain marshes in Arizona all provide mixed habitat where birds thrive.

Begin the route in Eagar as you take Water Canyon Road to Big Lake, and return to your beginning along Arizona Routes 261 and 260.

Riparian growth attracts birders along with birds.

Birding information:

Red-winged and Yellow-headed Blackbirds, Belted Kingfisher, Great Blue Heron, and a variety of waterfowl can be seen along the water and marshlands here. Western Bluebird and Horned Lark can be seen in the open grassland, and various songbirds, including several species of woodpeckers, thrive in the ponderosa pine forests.

Additional help:

Elevation: Between 7,000 and 9,000 feet.

Hazards: Early or late snow.

Recreational Map of Arizona location: F9

Nearest food, gas, and lodging: Springerville and Eagar.

Camping: Campground at Big Lake, and primitive camping on national forest land.

Land ownership and/or contact: Apache-Sitgreaves National Forest, Springerville Ranger District.

Springerville and Big Lake loop

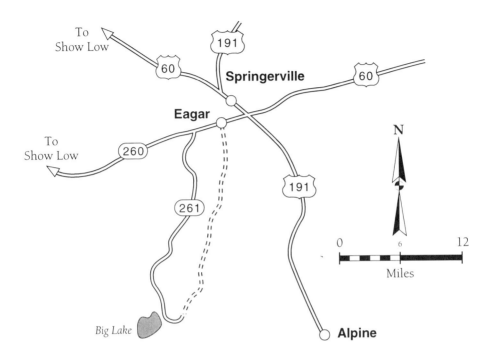

27. Escudilla Mountain and Terry Flat

Habitats: Spruce-fir forest, mountain meadows, open grasslands.

Key birds: Wild Turkey, Blue Grouse, Northern Goshawk, Broad-tailed Hummingbird, Mountain Bluebird, Western Tanager, and Yellow-rumped Warbler.

Best times to bird: Spring breeding season.

General information:

This is high country, with the loop around 10,877-foot Escudilla Mountain to Terry Flat over 9,000 feet, and the birds found here are those that gravitate to spruce-fir forest.

The drive from U.S. Highway 180 between Eagar and Alpine to the peak loop road is easy, and the viewing is excellent as the road winds around the peak where wildflowers abound in July and August.

Escudilla Mountain and Terry Flat

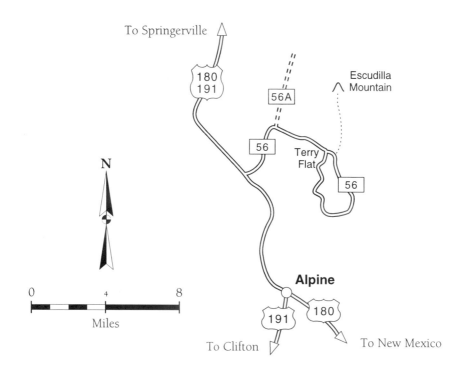

There is a 3-mile-long trail to the top of the peak from Terry Flat for the more adventurous birders.

Birding information:

Blue Grouse, Dark-eyed Junco, Western Tanager, and Mountain Bluebird inhabit the forest, and Northern Goshawk hunt in the high meadows.

Additional help:

> **Elevation:** Between 8,000 and 10,000 feet.
>
> **Hazards:** Early or late snow.
>
> **Recreational Map of Arizona location:** F9
>
> **Nearest food, gas, and lodging:** Alpine.
>
> **Camping:** At Forest Service campgrounds at Luna Lake (off US 180) and Alpine.
>
> **Land ownership and/or contact:** Apache-Sitgreaves National Forest, Alpine Ranger District.

Red-tailed Hawks frequently alight on top of utility poles alongside the highway.

28. Eagle Creek and Honeymoon Campground ——

Habitats: Grasslands, juniper-oak woodlands, ponderosa pine forest, and riparian woodlands.

Key birds: Bald Eagle, Great Blue Heron, Northern Flicker, and several hummingbird species.

Best times to bird: During spring migration and breeding season.

General information:

Eagle Creek flows through thick riparian woodlands surrounded by open grasslands and juniper-oak forest. Birders enjoy this isolated site as they drive along the 12 miles of dirt road from U.S. Highway 191 (The Coronado Trail) to the Honeymoon Campground at the end of the road.

Eagle Creek and Honeymoon Campground;
Bonita Creek

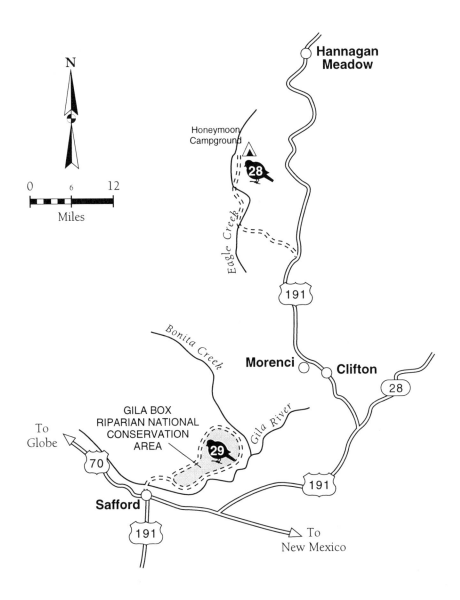

Birding information:

American Kestrel and Red-tailed Hawk hunt in the grasslands adjacent to the road, and several Bald Eagle winter along the creek. Spring migration brings plenty of songbirds into the area, and during the summer you can see Northern Flicker in the forest and several species of hummingbirds in the meadows.

Come in the early spring and watch the Great Blue Heron build their nests, present their courtship displays, and feed their young at two rookeries atop tall cottonwood trees near the creek.

Additional help:

Elevation: About 6,500 feet.

Hazards: Early or late snow.

Recreational Map of Arizona location: G9

Nearest food, gas, and lodging: Stargo, Morenci, and Clifton.

Camping: At a campground at the site.

Land ownership and/or contact: Apache-Sitgreaves National Forest, Clifton Ranger District.

29. Bonita Creek

Habitats: Riparian woodlands in desert canyon.

Key birds: Gambel's Quail, Summer Tanager, Yellow-billed Cuckoo, Common Black-Hawk, Zone-tailed Hawk, and Canyon Wren.

Best times to bird: Spring breeding season.

General information:

The creosote-bush desert above Bonita Creek Canyon is drab and rather lifeless. Birds thrive in the canyon below, where scattered stands of cottonwood and sycamore provide food and shelter. In 1990, Bonita Creek and part of the Gila River were included in the Gila Box Riparian National Conservation Area to protect this important birding area.

The area is located in wildlands between Safford and Morenci where few roads lead, and those that do are not very well maintained.

Birding information:

Almost 150 species of birds have been reported in the canyon, and more than 70 have been reported as nesting there.

Spring migration offers the best opportunity for seeing large numbers of species such as Summer Tanager, Yellow-billed Cuckoo, Common Black-Hawk, and Zone-tailed Hawk.

The Central Mountain region is home to many raptors, such as this Swainson's Hawk.

Additional help:

Elevation: Between 2,000 and 3,000 feet.

Hazards: High summer heat and rough roads.

Recreational Map of Arizona location: H9

Nearest food, gas, and lodging: Safford.

Camping: Primitive camping on BLM lands and developed campground at Roper Lake State Park south of Safford.

Land ownership and/or contact: Bureau of Land Management, Gila Resource Area.

Southeastern Arizona
Sky Islands

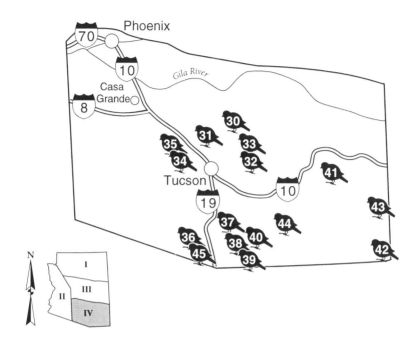

This lonely road leads into a true mecca for birders, Cave Creek Canyon.

30. Aravaipa Canyon

Habitats: Riparian woodlands, steep cliffs, and open desert.

Key birds: Gray and Zone-tailed Hawks, Common Black-Hawk, Blue Grosbeak, Yellow Warbler, Buff-collared Nightjar, Peregrine Falcon, Bell's Vireo, Northern Beardless Tyrannulet, and Mississippi Kite (at nearby Dudleyville).

Best times to bird: Spring migration and breeding season.

General information:

Aravaipa Canyon cuts through the Galiuro Mountains about 50 miles north of Tucson, and 10 miles of the central gorge is a wilderness area. On both ends of the wilderness area, The Nature Conservancy maintains the Aravaipa Canyon Preserve.

The canyon walls reach over 1,000 feet above Aravaipa Creek at spots, and over 230 species of birds have been reported in the gorge.

Aravaipa Canyon

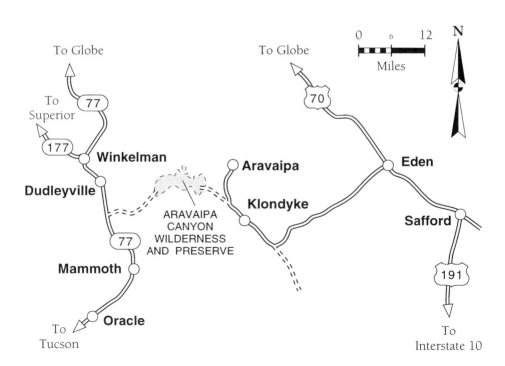

Only a lucky few get to see the reclusive Buff-collared Nightjar.

Access to this pristine area is limited, and information about permits can be obtained from both TNC and BLM.

Birding information:

A long list of rare, endangered, or just hard-to-find birds inhabits Aravaipa Canyon for at least part of the year. If you are lucky enough to obtain a permit to bird in the canyon you are sure to add to your life list.

Additional help:

Elevation: Between 2,500 and 3,500 feet.

Hazards: High summer heat and rough roads.

Recreational Map of Arizona location: H7

Nearest food, gas, and lodging: Safford to the east, and Dudleyville to the west.

Camping: At Fourmile Canyon Campground at Klondyke and several Forest Service campgrounds in the Pinaleño Mountains above Fort

Grant to the east. Primitive camping on BLM lands at Turkey Creek, also on the east side.

Land ownership and/or contact: Aravaipa Canyon Preserve, and Bureau of Land Management, Safford District Office.

31. Catalina State Park

Habitats: Sonoran Desert with mesquite bosque, paloverde trees, and saguaro cactus stands.

Key birds: Crissal and Bendire's Thrashers, Lucy's Warbler, Cactus Wren, Pyrrhuloxia, Blue Grosbeak, Abert's Towhee, Northern Beardless-Tyrannulet, various types of buntings, Elf Owl, Buff-collared Nightjar, and Rufous-crowned Sparrow.

Best times to bird: Spring migration and breeding season, and winter for migrants.

Catalina State Park; Sabino Canyon Recreation Area; Mount Lemmon drive; Saguaro National Monument; Arizona-Sonora Desert Museum

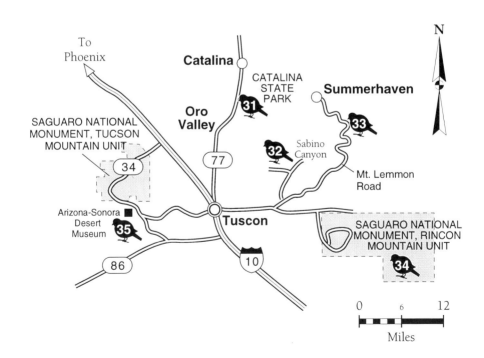

Pyrrhuloxia are found regularly around Tucson. This one was photographed at Sabino Canyon.

General information:

This state park is located on the outskirts of Tucson where housing divisions have pushed to its very boundaries. That does not make it any less of a birding site, though, for the lands within the park are home to a good selection of both desert and low mountain birds.

Many birders stay in comfort in Tucson and visit the park to bird in the early morning and late evening.

Birding information:

The list of birds above indicates the importance of Catalina State Park as a "don't miss" stop for any birder visiting southeastern Arizona and the Sky Islands.

Additional help:

Elevation: Between 2,700 and 6,000 feet.

Hazards: High summer heat and rattlesnakes.

Recreational Map of Arizona location: 16

Nearest food, gas, and lodging: Tucson and its northern suburbs.

Camping: At campground in park.

Land ownership and/or contact: Catalina State Park.

32. Sabino Canyon Recreation Area

Habitats: Desert canyon with riparian growth.

Key birds: White-winged Dove, White-throated Swift, Gila and Ladder-backed Woodpeckers, Brown-crested Flycatcher, Hooded and Scott's Orioles, Cactus, Canyon, and Rock Wrens, Curve-billed and Crissal Thrashers, Phainopepla, Pyrrhuloxia, Lesser Goldfinch, Greater Roadrunner, and Elf Owl.

Best times to bird: Spring migration and breeding season, and winter for migrants.

General information:

This popular recreation site outside Tucson offers easy access to birders who want to ride a tram and watch for birds along the sides of the road.

For those who wish to be a little more adventurous, trails lead up both Sabino and Bear canyons, where birds are very active.

Try to avoid weekends here, though, for the 30,000 or 40,000 other visitors may hamper your birding.

Birding information:

Begin at the visitor center, where exhibits indicate the best sites to view birds and a cactus garden attracts a number of birds. Rangers lead guided bird walks almost daily, and these are a great introduction to the bird life in the canyon.

Additional help:

Elevation: Between 2,800 and 3,400 feet.

Hazards: High summer heat and rattlesnakes.

Recreational Map of Arizona location: 17

Nearest food, gas, and lodging: Tucson and its eastern suburbs.

Camping: At Forest Service campgrounds on Mount Lemmon Road.

Land ownership and/or contact: Sabino Canyon Recreation Area, Coronado National Forest, Santa Catalina Ranger District.

33. Mount Lemmon drive ───────────────

Habitats: Four life zones, from low desert scrub to Canadian, are located along the 40 miles of this road from Tucson to the top of Mount Lemmon.

Key birds: Gambel's Quail, Bridled Titmouse, Scott's Oriole, Strickland's Woodpecker, Painted Redstart, White-throated Swift, Greater Pewee, Red-faced Warbler, Pygmy Nuthatch, Zone-tailed Hawk, Cordilleran Flycatcher (a rare Mexican migrant), Virginia's Warbler, Yellow-eyed Junco, and Orange-crowned Warbler.

Best times to bird: Anytime of year is good somewhere along this route.

General information:

The road to the top of Mount Lemmon crosses all the major life zones found in the Sky Islands of Arizona; the route leads from the hot desert to cold mountain forests.

When making this trip, try to avoid weekends, and get an early start. Birding is best here in the early morning, and it is wise to slowly work your way up the mountain without hitting the extreme cold of early morning at the top of the road.

The many pullouts and rest stops on the way to the top provide excellent places to bird with the gains in elevation.

The visitor center at Palisades Ranger Station has excellent exhibits of the life zones and wildlife of Mount Lemmon, and a visit there will make it easier to locate birds.

Birding information:

This route offers the best chance of finding a number of birds particular to Arizona. If you have time for only one major birding trip while in the state, this is the one to choose.

Additional help:

Elevation: Between 2,000 and 9,000 feet.

Hazards: High summer heat and rattlesnakes at lower elevations; unseasonable snow at higher.

Recreational Map of Arizona location: 17

Nearest food, gas, and lodging: Summerhaven at the peak and Tucson suburbs to the south.

Camping: At Forest Service campgrounds at a number of sites along the road to the top.

Land ownership and/or contact: Coronado National Forest, Santa Catalina Ranger District.

34. Saguaro National Monument

Habitats: Open desert and saguaro forest.

Key birds: Gilded and Gila Woodpeckers, Elf Owl, Western Screech-Owl, Cactus Wren, Crissal, Sage, and Curve-billed Thrashers, Lucy's Warbler, Pyrrhuloxia, Harris' Hawk, Bell's Vireo, Rufous-winged Sparrow, White-winged Dove, Verdin, Vermilion Flycatcher, Phainopepla, Greater Roadrunner, and Scott's Oriole.

Best times to bird: All year, but summers can be very hot.

The Gila Woodpecker is a familiar sight around stands of saguaro cactus.

General information:

The two large units of this national monument, Tucson Mountain and Rincon Mountain, are located on opposite sides of Tucson, and if you are short of time head for the Tucson Mountain Unit on the west.

There you can bird among the stands of saguaro cactus and visit the Arizona-Sonora Desert Museum (see next entry) on the same visit.

Birding information:

Almost all the low desert birds are reported here, and this is the best chance to see most of them.

Large saguaros provide food and shelter for a multitude of wildlife. Northern (Gilded) Flicker and Gila Woodpecker excavate holes in the tall cacti for nesting sites. Once they leave, the cavities are taken over by Elf Owl and Western Screech-Owl, as well as Cactus Wren and Lucy's Warbler.

As the tall saguaro bloom, keep an eye out for White-winged Dove feeding on the nectar in the blooms as well as the seeds that develop afterward.

Additional help:

Elevation: Between 2,600 and 5,000 feet.

Hazards: High summer heat, lack of water, rough roads, and rattlesnakes.

Recreational Map of Arizona location: 16, 17

Nearest food, gas, and lodging: Tucson and its suburbs.

Camping: In Tucson Mountain Park near the western unit of the national monument.

Land ownership and/or contact: Saguaro National Monument.

35. Arizona-Sonora Desert Museum ————————

Habitats: Sonoran Desert.

Key birds: All of those listed for the Saguaro National Monument, plus some migrants drawn by feeders. There is also an enclosed aviary where many native birds may be viewed. This exhibit changes by seasons.

Best times to bird: Any time of the year, but summers can be very hot.

General information:

This museum-zoo has long been recognized as one of the top ten zoos in the world, and if you are in the area don't miss a trip here. Not only does it have outstanding exhibits of desert wildlife and plants, but it has two premier aviaries. One is for hummingbirds only, and all of the species reported in Arizona are exhibited here at some time during the year. The exhibit is changed seasonally according to the migration patterns of the various species.

Gila Woodpecker.

The other aviary features songbirds of Arizona, and these exhibits are also changed seasonally to showcase the birds most likely to be seen in the outdoors at any given time.

Birding information:

The gardens of the museum attract many resident birds, and it is not unusual to see a bird in the aviary and later spot it in the garden outside.

Docents in the aviaries can provide good advice to birders about where in the Tucson area various hard-to-find species have recently been reported.

Additional help:

Elevation: About 3,000 feet.

Hazards: High summer heat.

Recreational Map of Arizona location: I6

Scattered stands of mesquite break up the open grasslands of the Buenos Aires National Wildlife Refuge.

Nearest food, gas, and lodging: Tucson and its suburbs.

Camping: In Tucson Mountain Park nearby.

Land ownership and/or contact: Arizona-Sonora Desert Museum.

36. Buenos Aires National Wildlife Refuge

Habitats: Open grasslands, mesquite bosque, riparian woodlands, marsh, and lake.

Key birds: Northern (Masked) Bobwhite, Scaled, Gambel's, and Montezuma Quails, Swainson's Hawk, Horned Lark, Botteri's, Cassin's, and Grasshopper Sparrows, Vermilion Flycatcher, Summer Tanager, Gray Hawk, and Tropical Kingbird.

Best times to bird: Any time of the year, but best times are during spring breeding and migration season and during the fall.

General information:

The grasslands of this refuge are the largest ungrazed section of grasslands in Arizona, although they have been grazed extensively in the past. Today the refuge is home to a wide range of wildlife and offers at least two very distinct birding habitats. The first is the open grasslands that include most of the refuge acreage, and the second is the riparian woodlands along Arivaca Creek on the northeastern edge of the refuge.

Buenos Aires National Wildlife Refuge

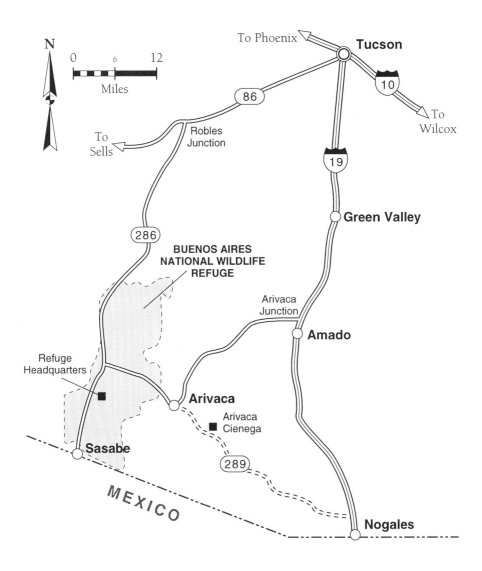

Another habitat administered by the refuge is the wetlands at Arivaca Cienega, which is located some distance to the east of the main refuge lands.

Birding information:

This is the only spot in the United States to see Northern (Masked) Bobwhite, and Scaled, Montezuma, and Gambel's Quail within a short distance of each other. The Masked Bobwhite have been reintroduced into the area in the recent past, and the refuge is continuing to breed this rare bird and plant adults until a sustainable population is reached.

The birding around Arivaca Creek is very different from that of the open grasslands of the refuge. In the riparian growth, look for Summer Tanager, Vermilion Flycatcher, Northern Cardinal, and other colorful songbirds. Gray Hawk also nest in the cottonwood here.

Additional help:

Elevation: Between 3,200 and 4,800 feet.

Hazards: Rough roads.

Recreational Map of Arizona location: J6

Nearest food, gas, and lodging: Sasabe and Arivaca, and Arivaca Junction.

Camping: Primitive camping at specified sites on refuge.

Land ownership and/or contact: Buenos Aires National Wildlife Refuge.

Birding is great around San Xavier del Bac Mission south of Tucson, where you can find Bendire's and Crissal Thrashers.

37. Madera Canyon and Florida Wash

Habitats: Desert canyon, oak woodlands, riparian woodlands, and ponderosa pine forest.

Key birds: Elegant Trogon, Buff-collared Nightjar, Sulphur-bellied Flycatcher, Summer Tanager, Bridled Titmouse, Northern Beardless-Tyrannulet, Bells' Vireo, Scaled Quail, Crissal Thrasher, Pyrrhuloxia, Phianopepla, Rufous-winged Sparrow, Band-tailed Pigeon, Painted Redstart, Chipping Sparrow, Hepatic Tanager, Hooded, Northern, and Scott's Orioles, Flammulated Owl, Whiskered Screech-Owl, Common Poorwill, Whip-poor-will, and Elf Owl. Fifteen different species of hummingbirds have been reported in the canyon, the most of any spot in the United States.

Best times to bird: Any time of the year, but best in spring and fall.

General information:

Florida (pronounced Flow-REE-da) Wash is desert country where song-birds can be found in abundance. As you drive higher into Madera Canyon the landscape becomes mixed conifer forests and the bird population is dramatically different even though you have gone only 12 or so miles.

Santa Rita Lodge is located midway up Madera Canyon, and if there is a birding mecca in the nation, it is here. Birders from around the world

Birding is good in Florida Wash at the base of Madera Canyon.

Madera Canyon and Florida Wash; Patagonia-Sonoita Creek Preserve; San Pedro Riparian National Conservation Area; Ramsey Canyon and Carr Canyon; Empire/Cienega Resource Conservation Area

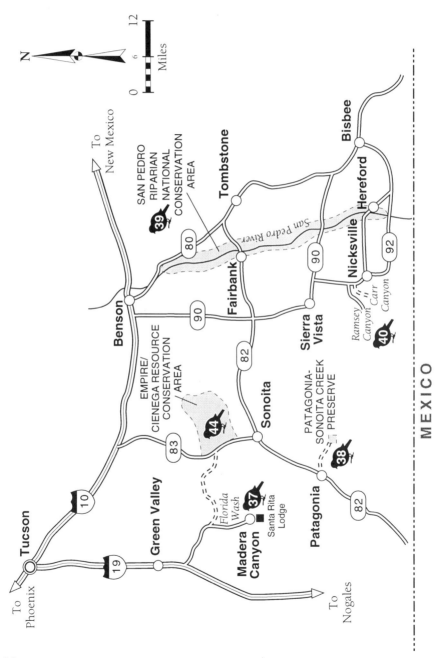

Santa Rita Lodge is visited by birders from around the world, and its courtyard is a great place to watch for birds as you relax.

congregate at the feeders in the lodge's court to look for elusive species that are difficult to find elsewhere.

Birding information:

The list of birds recorded here matches that of any other site in the country. From the seldom-seen Buff-collared Nightjar to the Elegant Trogon, birders find new additions to their life lists on every visit here.

Though it is easy to see a number of birds at the feeders, more energetic birders hike up the Mount Wrightson Trail in search of the nesting Elegant Trogon.

Hummingbirds also are well represented in the canyon, and almost as many are reported here each season as at Ramsey Canyon to the east.

Additional help:

Elevation: Between 3,000 and 9,500 feet.

Hazards: Unseasonable snow at higher elevations.

Recreational Map of Arizona location: J7

Nearest food, gas, and lodging: Green Valley.

Camping: At campground in the canyon.

Land ownership and/or contact: Coronado National Forest, Nogales Ranger District.

38. Patagonia-Sonoita Creek Preserve ───────

Habitats: Riparian woodlands.

Key birds: Gray Hawk, Vermilion Flycatcher, Great Blue Heron, Rose-throated Becard, Ground Dove, Gray-breasted Jay, Bridled Titmouse, Verdin, Bewick's Wren, Band-tailed Pigeon, Cassin's, Thick-billed, and Western Kingbirds, Summer Tanager, Blue Grosbeak, Yellow-billed Sapsucker, Green-tailed Towhee, Dark-eyed Junco, and Lincoln's Sparrow.

Best times to bird: Any time of the year. During migration you can see more species here than almost anywhere else in the state.

General information:

This Nature Conservancy preserve to the northeast of Nogales includes some of the best and most pristine riparian habitat in the state. Joseph Wood Krutch once said of Sonoita Creek, "No other area in Arizona is more deserving of preservation."

The thousands of birders who visit the preserve each year all agree that the preservation of the area has added immeasurably to birding in southeastern Arizona.

Birding information:

Of the over 260 species reported here, some of the most sought after by birders include Green Kingfisher, Thick-billed Kingbird, Northern Beardless-Tyrannulet, and Rose-throated Becard.

Guided tours of the preserve are offered every Saturday, and additional walks and programs are given seasonally.

Additional help:

Elevation: About 4,000 feet.

Hazards: Few.

Recreational Map of Arizona location: J7

Nearest food, gas, and lodging: Patagonia and Sonoita.

Camping: At Parker Canyon and Patagonia Lake state parks.

Land ownership and/or contact: Patagonia-Sonoita Creek Preserve.

39. San Pedro Riparian National Conservation Area

Habitats: River bottomlands and riparian woodlands.

Key birds: Raptors abound here. Gray and Swainson's Hawks, Crested Caracara, and Mississippi Kite join Mallard, Mexican Duck, Green Kingfisher, Lark Bunting, Common Ground-Dove, Scaled Quail, Ladder-backed Woodpecker, Barn Owl, Yellow-billed Cuckoo, Northern Cardinal, Yellow-breasted Chat, Summer Tanager, and Blue Grosbeak.

Best times to bird: March through September.

General information:

A 40-mile-long stretch of the San Pedro River north from the Mexican border has been preserved in this conservation area, and it offers outstanding birding opportunities.

There has been little development or intrusion into the riparian woodlands along the river, and birders who want to explore here have plenty of opportunities to walk alone through tall stands of willow, cottonwood, and sycamore where 379 species of birds have been reported. More than 100 of these are known to nest in the area.

Birding information:

There are limited access points to this long corridor, and which one to choose depends upon what birds you wish to find. Contact the conservation area headquarters for information about the location of various species, and the best access points to see them.

Scaled Quail are one of four species found in southeastern Arizona. The others are Masked Bobwhite, Montezuma, and Gambel's Quail.

Additional help:

Elevation: About 4,000 feet.

Hazards: Few.

Recreational Map of Arizona location: J8

Nearest food, gas, and lodging: Sierra Vista, Hereford, Fairbank, Tombstone, and Bisbee.

Camping: In Coronado National Forest to the west.

Land ownership and/or contact: San Pedro Riparian National Conservation Area.

40. Ramsey Canyon and Carr Canyon

Habitats: Wooded mountain canyons.

Key birds: Hummingbirds are the prime feature here, with more than fifteen species regularly seen. Other birds include Buff-breasted Flycatcher, Strickland's Woodpecker, and Olive and Red-faced Warblers.

Best times to bird: From spring breeding season through September.

General information:

This is another Nature Conservancy preserve, and one that is world-famous for its hummingbird feeders, where more than fifteen species of hummers are seen each year.

The preserve's reputation has its downside, though, for you must come early if you want to get in. Since it is only 6 miles from Sierra Vista, birders can find food and lodging nearby and drive into the preserve early in the morning. Reservations are required for weekends and holidays.

There are 6 cabins on site that TNC rents, but these also must be reserved well in advance.

A good alternative to Ramsey Canyon is to take the rough road into nearby Carr Canyon to see many of the same birds, but without the crowds.

Birding information:

In addition to the many species of hummingbirds that are a major attraction for birders, there are a number of other rare or hard-to-find birds that have been reported at Ramsey and Carr canyons. These include Strickland's Woodpecker, Olive and Red-faced Warblers, and Buff-breasted Flycatcher.

Additional help:

Elevation: Between 5,500 and 7,500 feet.

Hazards: Rough roads and unseasonable snow.

Recreational Map of Arizona location: J7, J8

Nearest food, gas, and lodging: Sierra Vista.

Camping: At undeveloped campground in top of Carr Canyon.

Land ownership and/or contact: Coronado National Forest, Sierra Vista Ranger District, and Ramsey Canyon Preserve.

Magnificent, Black-chinned, and Broad-tailed Hummingbirds (at top, bottom left, and bottom right) are just three of more than fifteen species regularly reported in southeastern Arizona.

41. Willcox Playa Wildlife Area

Habitats: Dry lake bed with some depressions and ponds with water.

Key birds: Sandhill Crane, Chihuahuan Raven, American Avocet, Burrowing Owl, Mountain Plover, and Sage Sparrow.

Best times to bird: Winter, spring, and fall. Summers are hot and dry.

Willcox Playa Wildlife Area; Guadalupe Canyon; Cave Creek Canyon and Rustler Park

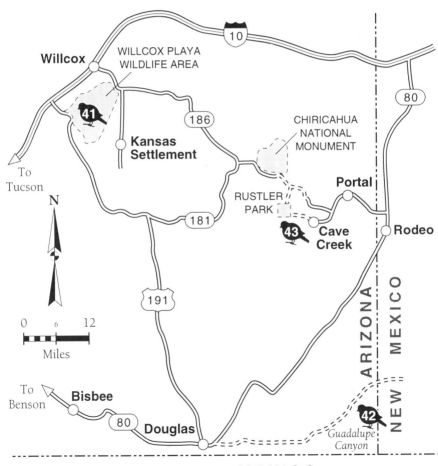

General information:

This large dry lake bed is a barren-looking site where one is surprised to find any wildlife, much less abundant bird life. Appearances are deceiving, however, and at various times of the year birding is excellent here.

Birding information:

More than 6,000 Sandhill Crane winter over in the playa where surrounding farms provide excellent food for both the crane and waterfowl that come when the winter rains fill the lake bed with several inches of water.

Hawks are also abundant in the region during the winter.

Additional help:

Elevation: About 4,000 feet.

Hazards: High summer heat and rattlesnakes.

Recreational Map of Arizona location: 18

Nearest food, gas, and lodging: Willcox.

Camping: In the Dragoon Mountains to the south.

Land ownership and/or contact: Arizona Game and Fish Department, Region 5.

42. Guadalupe Canyon

Habitats: Narrow canyon with riparian growth.

Key birds: Buff-collared Nightjar, Thick-billed Kingbird, Scrub Jay, Gray-breasted Jay, Summer Tanager, Black-headed and Blue Grosbeaks, Varied Bunting, Zone-tailed and Cooper's Hawks, Gila, Acorn, and Ladder-backed Woodpeckers, Violet-crowned Hummingbird, White-winged Dove, and Common Ground-Dove.

Best times to bird: From spring through late fall.

The Yellow Grosbeak is one of three grosbeaks seen in southeastern Arizona. The others are the Black-headed and Blue.

General information:

The attraction of this site is its inaccessibility. Located along the New Mexico-Arizona state line just north of the Mexican border, the canyon is one of the most difficult sites in this guide to reach. You must navigate 40 miles of dirt road to reach the canyon. Once there, the best birding is about a 4-mile hike into the canyon from the end of the road.

In recent years the new owners of the land around the canyon have begun to rehabilitate overgrazed lands, and ask that birders be aware of and respect these attempts.

Birding information:

Most of the birds found here are also found much closer to civilization, particularly around Tucson, so the vast majority of birders will spend their time watching birds in other areas rather than travel to this isolated corner of Arizona. Others, however, will delight in listening for the Buff-collared Nightjar, which was first discovered here in 1958; Common Poorwill; and Western Screech Owl as they sleep out under starry skies far from any cities.

Additional help:

Elevation: About 3,000 feet.

Hazards: Flash floods in summer, rough roads, and rattlesnakes.

Recreational Map of Arizona location: J9

Nearest food, gas, and lodging: Douglas.

Camping: Primitive camping in canyon. There has been some discussion of stopping this, so you may wish to check before heading into the area.

Land ownership and/or contact: Bureau of Land Management, Las Cruces District Office.

43. Cave Creek Canyon and Rustler Park ————————

Habitats: Desert grasslands, riparian woodlands, ponderosa pine forest, and high mountain meadows.

Key birds: Elegant Trogon, Blue Grosbeak, Painted Redstart, Sulphur-bellied Flycatcher, Prairie Falcon, Band-tailed Pigeon, Black Phoebe, Acorn, Ladder-backed, and Strickland's Woodpeckers, Gray-breasted Jay, Hooded and Scott's Orioles, Western and Whiskered Screech-Owls, Virginia's, Grace's, and Red-faced Warblers, Hepatic Tanager, Hairy Woodpecker, Red Crossbill, and Yellow-eyed Junco.

Best times to bird: Spring through fall.

The panoramic vistas of the Chiricahua Mountains are outstanding from the road to Rustler Park.

General information:

Aside from Madera Canyon, there is no other spot in Arizona that attracts more birders from around the world. Its distance from any population center keeps day birders from making the trip, as many do to Madera Canyon, but the campgrounds in Cave Creek and at Rustler Park higher up in the mountains are constantly full of birders from spring through fall.

While here, a "don't miss" is the Spoffords' backyard viewing area in Portal. Just ask for directions at the ranger station or store in Portal. Remember that this home is in a subdivision; the Spoffords and their neighbors ask that you respect their quiet community as you drive into the area. This means driving slowly and not attempting to drive large campers and motorhomes into the subdivision.

Birding information:

Elegant Trogon, Rose-throated Becard, Blue Grosbeak, Montezuma Quail, Painted Redstart, Hepatic Tanager. With birds such as these, you can't miss adding to your life list on a visit to this outstanding birding area, whether you spend your time in Cave Creek Canyon or higher up the mountains at Rustler Park.

While traveling from one area to the other, don't miss the Southwestern Research Station and its hummingbird feeders.

Additional help:

    Elevation: Between 4,600 and 9,800 feet.

    Hazards: Early or late snow.

    Recreational Map of Arizona location: I9

    Nearest food, gas, and lodging: Portal, AZ, and Rodeo, NM.

    Camping: At Forest Service campgrounds throughout the Chiricahua Mountains.

    Land ownership and/or contact: Coronado National Forest, Douglas Ranger District.

44. Empire/Cienega Resource Conservation Area ——

    Habitats: Open grasslands and riparian woodlands.

    Key birds: Gray Hawk, Yellow-breasted Chat, Green Kingfisher, Great Blue Heron, Montezuma Quail, White-tailed (Black-shouldered) Kite, and Burrowing Owl.

    Best times to bird: Spring through fall.

General information:

This relatively new management area just north of the community of Sonoita covers what was once a vast cattle ranch. The grasslands are now recovering from long periods of grazing, and pronghorn roam where cattle dominated not long ago.

Several year-round streams provide water for good riparian growth where many birds thrive, and few birders wander onto the land.

Birding information:

Head for the streams for the prime features here of Green Kingfisher and Gray Hawk, but don't forget to watch for Montezuma Quail along the way.

Additional help:

    Elevation: About 4,500 feet.

    Hazards: Rough roads and rattlesnakes.

    Recreational Map of Arizona location: J7

    Nearest food, gas, and lodging: Sonoita.

    Camping: Primitive camping on conservation area land, and at Forest Service campgrounds in the Santa Rita Mountains to the west.

    Land ownership and/or contact: Empire/Cienega Resource Conservation Area, Bureau of Land Management, Tucson Resource Area.

45. Sycamore Canyon loop

Habitats: Riparian woodlands in deep canyon.

Key birds: Elegant Trogon, Rose-throated Becard, Five-striped Sparrow, Varied Bunting, and fifteen species of flycatchers.

Best times to bird: Year-round, but summers can be stifling hot.

General information:

This is for energetic birders who want to really get away from the crowds. First, you head south from Tucson toward Nogales on Interstate 19, and turn west 3 miles south of Rio Rico to Peña Blanca Lake. The pavement ends at the lake, and from there you continue another 9 miles on a rough dirt road to a sign that says Sycamore Canyon. Turn south at the sign and continue for another 0.5 mile to a parking area. From there it is a strenuous 2-mile hike down the canyon to the best birding sites.

Sycamore Canyon loop

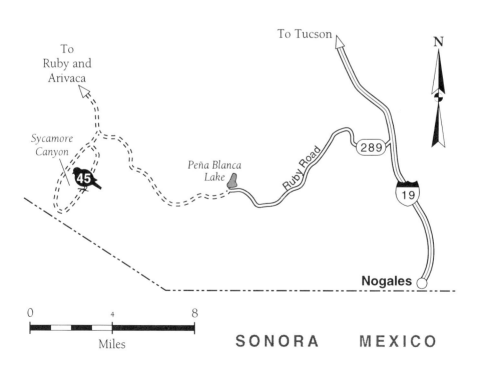

Birding information:

Fifteen species of flycatchers have been spotted in the canyon. Elegant Trogon have been reported far up the canyon and Rose-throated Becard farther down. Another rare species reported here is the Louisiana Waterthrush.

Be prepared for the canyon to be remarkably empty of birds, however, for at times birders report making the strenuous hike only to find no birds visible in the canyon. At other times there is an abundance of species present.

Additional help:

Elevation: Between 3,500 and 4,000 feet.

Hazards: High summer heat, lack of water, rattlesnakes, and isolation.

Recreational Map of Arizona location: J6

Nearest food, gas, and lodging: Nogales.

Camping: At Peña Blanca Lake Recreation Area.

Land ownership and/or contact: Coronado National Forest, Nogales Ranger District.

The Common Raven can be seen throughout the desert country where it frequently rests atop tall cactus arms.

CHAPTER 4

Checklist, seasonal occurrence, and abundance of Arizona birds

Approximately 414 species of birds have been documented in Arizona, and another 50 species are historicals or accidentals. The following checklist of Arizona birds includes distribution within the Northern (N), Southwest (SW), and Southeast (SE) regions of the state, and relative abundance in summer and winter. The birds found in the Central Mountain Region included in this guide may be from any of the three regions listed below. Check the overlapping areas to see which region you need to use.

Migrants are noted by an "M" after the species name, and nesting species are noted by an "N".

An asterisk after the species name indicates the Arizona Bird Committee desires documented sightings of this species to substantiate the species as an Arizona bird species.

SPECIES	REGION	Winter	Summer
Red-throated Loon* M	SW	· · · · · · · ·	· · · · · · · ·
Arctic Loon M	SE	· · · · · · · ·	· · · · · · · ·
	SW	· · · · · · · ·	· · · · · · · ·
	N	· · · · · · · ·	· · · · · · · ·
Common Loon M	SE	• • • • • • •	· · · · · · · ·
	SW		· · · · · · · ·
	N	• • • • • • •	· · · · · · · ·
Least Grebe* N	SE	· · · · · · · ·	· · · · · · · ·
	SW	· · · · · · · ·	· · · · · · · ·
Pied-billed Grebe N	SE	● ● ● ● ● ● ●	● ● ● ● ● ● ●
	SW	● ● ● ● ● ● ●	● ● ● ● ● ● ●
	N	· · · · · · · ·	● ● ● ● ● ● ●
Horned Grebe M	SE	· · · · · · · ·	· · · · · · · ·
	SW	• • • • • • •	· · · · · · · ·
	N	· · · · · · · ·	· · · · · · · ·
Eared Grebe N	SE	● ● ● ● ● ● ●	· · · · · · · ·
	SW	● ● ● ● ● ● ●	· · · · · · · ·
	N	· · · · · · · ·	● ● ● ● ● ● ●
Western Grebe N dark phase	SE	· · · · · · · ·	· · · · · · · ·
	SW	● ● ● ● ● ● ●	● ● ● ● ● ● ●
	N	• • • • • • •	• • • • • • •
Western Grebe N light phase	SW	● ● ● ● ● ● ●	● ● ● ● ● ● ●
Blue-footed Booby* M	SW	· · · · · · · ·	· · · · · · · ·
Brown Booby* M	SW	· · · · · · · ·	· · · · · · · ·
American White Pelican M	SE	· · · · · · · ·	· · · · · · · ·
	SW	• • • • • • •	• • • • • • •
	N	· · · · · · · ·	· · · · · · · ·

M = migrating species, N = nesting species

 * = The Arizona Bird Committee desires documented sightings of this species to substantiate the species as an Arizona bird species.

· · · · · · · · = Poor   • • • • • • • = Moderate   ● ● ● ● ● ● ● = Good

SPECIES	REGION	Winter	Summer
		Seasonal Occurence and Abundance	
Brown Pelican M	SE		Poor
	SW	Moderate	Moderate
	N		Poor
Double-crested Cormorant N	SE	Moderate	Moderate
	SW	Moderate	Moderate
	N	Poor	Poor
Olivaceous Cormorant M	SE	Poor	Poor
	SW	Poor	Poor
Magnificent Frigatebird M	SE	Poor	Poor
	SW		
American Bittern N	SE	Poor	
	SW	Moderate	Poor
	N		Poor
Least Bittern N	SE	Poor	
	SW	Moderate	Moderate
	N		Poor
Great Blue Heron N	SE	Moderate	Moderate
	SW	Moderate	Moderate
	N	Poor	Good
Great Egret N	SE	Poor	Moderate
	SW	Moderate	Moderate
	N		Poor
Snowy Egret N	SE	Poor	Moderate
	SW	Moderate	Good
	N	Poor	Moderate
Little Blue Heron M	SE		Poor
	SW		Poor
Tricolored Heron M	SE	Poor	Poor
	SW	Poor	Poor
	N	Poor	Poor
Reddish Egret* M	SW	Poor	Poor

M = migrating species, N = nesting species

* = The Arizona Bird Committee desires documented sightings of this species to substantiate the species as an Arizona bird species.

· · · · · · · · = Poor   • • • • • • • = Moderate   ● ● ● ● ● ● ● = Good

SPECIES   REGION   Seasonal Occurence and Abundance

✔	SPECIES	REGION	Winter	Summer
☐	Cattle Egret M	SE		● ● ● ● ● ● ●
		SW	● ● ● ● ● ● ●	● ● ● ● ● ● ●
		N	· · · · · · ·	· · · · · · ·
☐	Green-backed Heron N	SE	● ● ● ● ● ● ●	● ● ● ● ● ● ●
		SW	● ● ● ● ● ● ●	● ● ● ● ● ● ●
☐	Black-crowned Night-Heron N	SE	● ● ● ● ● ● ●	● ● ● ● ● ● ●
		SW	● ● ● ● ● ● ●	● ● ● ● ● ● ●
		N		· · · · · · ·
☐	White Ibis* M	SW	· · · · · · ·	· · · · · · ·
☐	White-faced Ibis M	SE	• • • • • • •	• • • • • • •
		SW	• • • • • • •	· · · · · · ·
☐	Roseate Spoonbill M	SW		· · · · · · ·
☐	Wood Stork M	SE		· · · · · · ·
		SW		· · · · · · ·
		N		· · · · · · ·
☐	Fulvous Whistling-Duck* M	SW	· · · · · · ·	· · · · · · ·
☐	Black-bellied Whistling-Duck M	SW	· · · · · · ·	• • • • • • • ● ● ● ● ● ● ●
☐	Tundra Swan M	SE	· · · · · · ·	
		SW	● ● ● ● ● ● ●	
		N	· · · · · · ·	· · · · · · ·
☐	Great White-fronted Goose M	SE	· · · · · · ·	
		SW	• • • • • • •	
		N	· · · · · · ·	
☐	Snow Goose M	SE	· · · · · · ·	
		SW	● ● ● ● ● ● ●	

M = migrating species,   N = nesting species

* = The Arizona Bird Committee desires documented sightings of this species to substantiate the species as an Arizona bird species.

· · · · · · · = Poor   • • • • • • • = Moderate   ● ● ● ● ● ● ● = Good

SPECIES ✔	REGION	Seasonal Occurence and Abundance	
		Winter	Summer
Ross' Goose M	SE	· · · · · · · ·	
	SW	· · · · · · ·	
Brant M	SE	· · · · · · ·	
	SW ·	· · · · · · ·	
Canada Goose M	SE	· · · · · · ·	
	SW	• • • • • • •	· · · · · · · ·
	N	· · · · · · · ·	• • • • • • •
Wood Duck M	SE		
	SW	• • • • • • •	· · · · · · ·
	N		· · · · · · ·
Green-winged Teal N	SE	• • • • • • •	· · · · · · ·
	SW	• • • • • • •	· · · · · · ·
	N	• • • • • • •	· · · · · · ·
Mallard N	SE	• • • • • • •	• • • • • • • •
	SW	• • • • • • •	• • • • • • •
	N	• • • • • • •	• • • • • • •
Mexican Duck N	SE	· · · · · · ·	· · · · · · ·
Northern Pintail N	SE	• • • • • • •	· · · · · · ·
	SW	• • • • • • •	· · · · · · ·
	N	· · · · · · ·	• • • • • • •
Blue-winged Teal N	SE		· · · · · · ·
	SW	• • • • • • •	· · · · · · ·
	N	· · · · · · ·	· · · · · · ·
Cinnamon Teal N	SE	· · · · · · ·	• • • • • • •
	SW	· · · · · · ·	• • • • • • •
	N		• • • • • • •
Northern Shoveler M	SE	• • • • • • •	· · · · · · ·
	SW	• • • • • • •	· · · · · · ·
	N	· · · · · · ·	· · · · · · ·
Gadwall N	SE	· · · · · · ·	· · · · · · ·
	SW	· · · · · · ·	• • • • • • •
	N	• • • • • • •	• • • • • • •

M = migrating species,   N = nesting species

* = The Arizona Bird Committee desires documented sightings of this species to substantiate the species as an Arizona bird species.

· · · · · · · · = Poor   • • • • • • = Moderate   ● ● ● ● ● ● = Good

✔	SPECIES	REGION	Winter	Summer
☐	Eurasian Wigeon M	SE	· · · · · · ·	· · · · · · ·
		SW	· · · · · · ·	· · · · · · ·
☐	American Wigeon N	SE	●●●●●●●	· · · · · · ·
		SW	●●●●●●●	· · · · · · ·
		N	· · · · · · ·	· · · · · · ·
☐	Canvasback M	SE	●●●●●●●	· · · · · · ·
		SW	●●●●●●●	· · · · · · ·
		N	· · · · · · ·	· · · · · · ·
☐	Redhead N	SE	●●●●●●●	
		SW	●●●●●●●	• • • • • • •
		N	· · · · · · ·	• • • • • • •
☐	Ring-necked Duck N	SE	●●●●●●●	· · · · · · ·
		SW	●●●●●●●	· · · · · · ·
		N	· · · · · · ·	●●●●●●●
☐	Greater Scaup M	SE	· · · · · · ·	
		SW	●●●●●●●	
☐	Lesser Scaup M	SE	●●●●●●●	· · · · · · ·
		SW	●●●●●●●	· · · · · · ·
		N	· · · · · · ·	• • • • • • •
☐	Oldsquaw* M	SE	· · · · · · ·	· · · · · · ·
		SW	· · · · · · ·	
☐	Black Scoter* M	SE	· · · · · · ·	· · · · · · ·
		SW	· · · · · · ·	· · · · · · ·
		N	· · · · · · ·	· · · · · · ·
☐	Surf Scoter M	SE	· · · · · · ·	· · · · · · ·
		SW	· · · · · · ·	· · · · · · ·
		N	· · · · · · ·	· · · · · · ·
☐	White-winged Scoter* M	SE	• • • • • •	· · · · · · ·
		SW	· · · · · · ·	· · · · · · ·
		N	· · · · · · ·	· · · · · · ·
☐	Common Goldeneye M	SE	· · · · · · ·	
		SW	●●●●●●●	
		N		• • • • • • •

M = migrating species,   N = nesting species

* = The Arizona Bird Committee desires documented sightings of this species to substantiate the species as an Arizona bird species.

· · · · · · · = Poor   • • • • • • • = Moderate   ●●●●●●● = Good

✔	SPECIES	REGION	Winter	Summer
	Barrow's Goldeneye M	SE	Poor	
		SW	Moderate	
	Bufflehead M	SE	Good	Poor
		SW	Good	Poor
		N		Moderate
	Hooded Merganser M	SE	Good	Poor
		SW	Good	Poor
		N	Poor	Poor
	Common Merganser N	SE	Poor	Moderate
		SW	Good	Poor
		N	Poor	Moderate
	Red-breasted Merganser M	SE	Poor	Moderate
		SW	Good	Poor
		N	Poor	Poor
	Ruddy Duck N	SE	Good	Good
		SW	Good	Good
		N	Poor	Good
	Black Vulture N	SE	Poor	Poor
		SW	Moderate	Moderate
	Turkey Vulture N	SE	Poor	Good
		SW	Good	Good
		N	Good	Good
	Osprey N	SE	Good	Poor
		SW	Good	Moderate
		N		Poor
	Black-shouldered Kite* N	SE	Poor	Poor
		SW	Poor	Poor
	Mississippi Kite N	SE		Moderate
		SW		Poor
	Bald Eagle N	SE	Poor	Moderate
		SW	Good	Poor
		N	Good	Poor

M = migrating species,   N = nesting species
 * = The Arizona Bird Committee desires documented sightings of this species to substantiate the species as an Arizona bird species.

· · · · · · · · = Poor   • • • • • • • = Moderate   ●●●●●●● = Good

SPECIES	REGION	Winter	Summer
Northern Harrier N	SE	Good	
	SW	Good	Poor
	N	Good	Poor
Sharp-shinned Hawk N	SE	Good	Poor
	SW	Good	
	N	Good	Good
Cooper's Hawk N	SE	Good	Good
	SW	Good	Good
	N	Poor	Good
Northern Goshawk N	SE	Good	Good
	SW	Poor	
	N	Good	Good
Common Black-Hawk N	SE		Poor
	SW		Poor
	N		Poor
Harris' Hawk N	SE	Good	Good
	SW	Good	Good
Gray Hawk N	SE	Poor	Poor
	SW	Poor	Poor
Red-shouldered Hawk* N	SE	Poor	Poor
	SW	Poor	Poor
Broad-winged Hawk* M	SE	Poor	Poor
	SW	Poor	Poor
Swainson's Hawk N	SE		Good
	SW	Poor	Poor
	N		Good
Zone-tailed Hawk N	SE		Good
	SW	Poor	Poor
	N		Good
Red-tailed Hawk N	SE	Good	Good
	SW	Good	Good
	N	Good	Good

M = migrating species, N = nesting species

* = The Arizona Bird Committee desires documented sightings of this species to substantiate the species as an Arizona bird species.

· · · · · · · = Poor   • • • • • • = Moderate   ● ● ● ● ● ● ● = Good

✔	Species	Region	Winter	Summer
☐	Ferruginous Hawk N	SE	• • • • • • •	
		SW	• • • • • • •	
		N	• • • • • • •	• • • • • • •
☐	Rough-legged Hawk M	SE	• • • • • • •	
		SW	• • • • • • •	
		N	• • • • • • •	
☐	Golden Eagle N	SE	• • • • • • •	• • • • • • •
		SW	• • • • • • •	• • • • • • •
		N	• • • • • • •	• • • • • • •
☐	Crested Caracara N	SE	· · · · · · ·	· · · · · · ·
		SW	• • • • • • •	• • • • • • •
		N	· · · · · · ·	· · · · · · ·
☐	American Kestrel N	SE	• • • • • • •	• • • • • • •
		SW	• • • • • • •	• • • • • • •
		N	• • • • • • •	• • • • • • •
☐	Merlin M	SE	• • • • • • •	
		SW	• • • • • • •	
		N	• • • • • • •	
☐	Peregrine Falcon N	SE	· · · · · · ·	· · · · · · ·
		SW	· · · · · · ·	· · · · · · ·
				· · · · · · ·
☐	Prairie Falcon N	SE	• • • • • • •	• • • • • • •
		SW	• • • • • • •	• • • • • • •
		N	• • • • • • •	• • • • • • •
☐	Chukar N	N	• • • • • •	• • • • • •
☐	Ring-necked Pheasant N	SE	· · · · · · ·	· · · · · · ·
		SW	· · · · · · ·	· · · · · · ·
		N	· · · · · · ·	· · · · · · ·
☐	Blue Grouse N	N	• • • • • • •	• • • • • • •
☐	Wild Turkey N	SE	• • • • • • •	• • • • • • •
		N	• • • • • • •	• • • • • • •

M = migrating species,   N = nesting species
* = The Arizona Bird Committee desires documented sightings of this species to substantiate the species as an Arizona bird species.

· · · · · · · = Poor   • • • • • • = Moderate   ●●●●●● = Good

SPECIES   REGION   Seasonal Occurence and Abundance

✔ Species	Region	Winter	Summer
Northern Masked Bobwhite N	SE	Poor	Poor
Montezuma Quail N	SE	Good	Good
	N	Poor	Poor
Scaled Quail N	SE	Good	Good
	N	Poor	Poor
Gambel's Quail N	SE	Good	Good
	SW	Good	Good
	N	Poor	Poor
Black Rail N	SW	Poor	Poor
Clapper Rail N	SW	Poor	Moderate
Virginia Rail N	SE	Good	Poor
	SW	Good	Poor
	N	Poor	Good
Sora N	SE	Good	Poor
	SW	Good	Poor
	N	Poor	Good
Purple Gallinule* M	SE	Poor	Poor
Common Moorhen N	SE	Good	Good
	SW	Good	Good
	N	Poor	Poor
American Coot N	SE	Good	Good
	SW	Good	Good
	N	Good	Good
Sandhill Crane M	SE	Good	
	SW	Good	

M = migrating species,　N = nesting species

* = The Arizona Bird Committee desires documented sightings of this species to substantiate the species as an Arizona bird species.

· · · · · · · = Poor　　● ● ● ● ● ● ● = Moderate　　● ● ● ● ● ● ● = Good

SPECIES	REGION	Winter	Summer
Seasonal Occurence and Abundance			
✔			
Black-bellied Plover M	SE		·········
	SW	·········	·········
	N		·········
Lesser Golden Plover M	SE		·········
	SW		·········
Snowy Plover N	SE	·········	·········
	SW	·········	·········
Semipalmated Plover M	SE		• • • • • • •
	SW		• • • • • • •
	N		• • • • • • •
Killdeer N	SE	● ● ● ● ● ● ●	● ● ● ● ● ● ●
	SW	● ● ● ● ● ● ●	● ● ● ● ● ● ●
	N	● ● ● ● ● ● ●	● ● ● ● ● ● ●
Mountain Plover M	SE	·········	
	SW	● ● ● ● ● ● ●	
Black-necked Stilt N	SE		• • • • • • •
	SW	● ● ● ● ● ● ●	● ● ● ● ● ● ●
	N	·········	·········
American Avocet N	SE	·········	·········
	SW	·········	● ● ● ● ● ● ●
	N	·········	·········
Greater Yellowlegs M	SE	·········	• • • • • • •
	SW	● ● ● ● ● ● ●	
	N		·········
Lesser Yellowlegs M	SE	·········	• • • • • • •
	SW	·········	• • • • • • •
	N		• • • • • • •
Solitary Sandpiper M	SE	• • • • • • •	
	SW	• • • • • • •	
	N	• • • • • • •	
Willet M	SE	• • • • • • •	
	SW	• • • • • • •	·········
	N	• • • • • • •	

M = migrating species,   N = nesting species
* = The Arizona Bird Committee desires documented sightings of this species to substantiate the species as an Arizona bird species.

········· = Poor   • • • • • • • = Moderate   ● ● ● ● ● ● ● = Good

SPECIES   REGION   Seasonal Occurence and Abundance

✔ Species	Region	Winter	Summer
Spotted Sandpiper N	SE	Good	
	SW	Good	
	N		Good
Whimbrel M	SE	Poor	Poor
	SW	Poor	Poor
Long-billed Curlew M	SE	Poor	Good
	SW	Poor	Moderate
	N		Moderate
Marbled Godwit M	SE	Moderate	Moderate
	SW	Moderate	Moderate
	N	Moderate	Moderate
Ruddy Turnstone M	SE	Poor	Poor
	SW	Poor	Poor
Red Knot M	SE	Poor	Poor
	SW	Poor	Poor
	N	Poor	Poor
Sanderling M	SE	Poor	Poor
	SW	Moderate	Moderate
	N	Poor	Poor
Semipalmated Sandpiper* M	SE	Poor	Poor
	SW	Poor	Poor
	N	Poor	Poor
Western Sandpiper M	SE	Poor	Moderate
	SW	Poor	Moderate
	N	Moderate	Moderate
Least Sandpiper M	SE	Good	
	SW	Good	
	N	Poor	Moderate
Baird's Sandpiper M	SE	Moderate	Moderate
	SW	Moderate	Moderate
	N	Moderate	Moderate
Pectoral Sandpiper M	SE	Moderate	Moderate
	SW	Moderate	Moderate
	N	Moderate	Moderate

M = migrating species,   N = nesting species

  * = The Arizona Bird Committee desires documented sightings of this species to substantiate the species as an Arizona bird species.

     · · · · · · · = Poor   • • • • • • • = Moderate   ●●●●●● = Good

SPECIES   REGION   Seasonal Occurence and Abundance

✔	Species	Region	Winter	Summer
☐	Dunlin M	SE	Poor	Poor
		SW	Poor	Poor
☐	Stilt Sandpiper M	SE	Moderate	Moderate
		SW	Moderate	Moderate
		N	Moderate	Moderate
☐	Short-billed Dowitcher M	SE	Poor	Poor
		SW	Moderate	Moderate
		N	Poor	Poor
☐	Long-billed Dowitcher M	SE	Poor	Moderate
		SW	Good	
		N	Moderate	Moderate
☐	Common Snipe N	SE	Good	
		SW	Good	
		N	Good	Moderate
☐	Wilson's Phalarope N	SE	Moderate	Moderate
		SW	Moderate	Moderate
		N	Moderate	Moderate
☐	Red-necked Phalarope M	SE	Moderate	Moderate
		SW	Moderate	Moderate
		N	Moderate	Moderate
☐	Red Phalarope M	SE	Poor	
		SW	Poor	
		N	Poor	
☐	Pomarine Jaeger* M	SW	Poor	
☐	Parasitic Jaeger* M	SW		
☐	Long-tailed Jaeger* M	SW	Poor	Poor
☐	Franklin's Gull M	SE	Moderate	Moderate
		SW	Poor	Poor
		N	Poor	Poor

M = migrating species, N = nesting species

  * = The Arizona Bird Committee desires documented sightings of this species to substantiate the species as an Arizona bird species.

· · · · · · · · = Poor   • • • • • • • = Moderate   ●●●●●●● = Good

SPECIES   REGION   Seasonal Occurence and Abundance

✔	Species	Region	Winter	Summer
☐	Bonaparte's Gull M	SE	Poor	Moderate
		SW	Poor	Moderate
		N	Moderate	Moderate
☐	Heermann's Gull M	SE	Poor	Poor
		SW	Poor	Poor
			Poor	Poor
☐	Ring-billed Gull	SE	Poor	Moderate
		SW	Good	Poor
		N	Poor	Moderate
☐	California Gull M	SE	Poor	Poor
		SW	Moderate	Moderate
		N	Poor	Poor
☐	Herring Gull M	SE	Poor	Poor
		SW	Good	Poor
		N	Poor	Poor
☐	Thayer's Gull* M	SE	Poor	Poor
		SW	Poor	Poor
		N	Poor	Poor
☐	Glaucous-winged Gull* M	SW	Poor	
☐	Black-legged Kittiwake* M	SE	Poor	Poor
		SW	Poor	Poor
☐	Sabine's Gull M	SW	Poor	Poor
			Poor	Poor
			Poor	Poor
☐	Caspian Tern M	SE	Poor	Poor
		SW	Moderate	Moderate
		N	Poor	Poor
☐	Common Tern M	SE	Poor	Poor
		SW	Moderate	Moderate
		N	Poor	Poor
☐	Arctic Tern* M	SE	Poor	Poor
		SW	Poor	Poor

M = migrating species, N = nesting species

   * = The Arizona Bird Committee desires documented sightings of this species to substantiate the species as an Arizona bird species.

· · · · · · · = Poor   • • • • • • • = Moderate   ●●●●●● = Good

✔ SPECIES	REGION	Winter	Summer
Forster's Tern M	SE	• • • • • • •	• • • • • • •
	SW	• • • • • • •	• • • • • • •
	N	• • • • • • •	• • • • • • •
Least Tern* M		· · · · · · ·	· · · · · · ·
		· · · · · · ·	· · · · · · ·
Flammulated Owl N	SE		● ● ● ● ● ● ●
	SW	· · · · · · ·	· · · · · · ·
	N		● ● ● ● ● ● ●
Western Screech-Owl N	SE	● ● ● ● ● ● ●	● ● ● ● ● ● ●
	SW	● ● ● ● ● ● ●	● ● ● ● ● ● ●
	N	● ● ● ● ● ● ●	● ● ● ● ● ● ●
Whiskered Screech-Owl N	SE	● ● ● ● ● ● ●	● ● ● ● ● ● ●
Great Horned Owl N	SE	● ● ● ● ● ● ●	● ● ● ● ● ● ●
	SW	● ● ● ● ● ● ●	● ● ● ● ● ● ●
	N	● ● ● ● ● ● ●	● ● ● ● ● ● ●
Northern Pygmy-Owl N	SE	● ● ● ● ● ● ●	● ● ● ● ● ● ●
	N	● ● ● ● ● ● ●	● ● ● ● ● ● ●
Ferruginous Pygmy-Owl N	SE	· · · · · · ·	· · · · · · ·
	SW	· · · · · · ·	· · · · · · ·
Elf Owl N	SE		● ● ● ● ● ● ●
	SW		● ● ● ● ● ● ●
Burrowing Owl N	SE	● ● ● ● ● ● ●	● ● ● ● ● ● ●
	SW	● ● ● ● ● ● ●	● ● ● ● ● ● ●
	N	· · · · · · ·	● ● ● ● ● ● ●
Spotted Owl N	SE	● ● ● ● ● ● ●	● ● ● ● ● ● ●
	N	● ● ● ● ● ● ●	● ● ● ● ● ● ●
Long-eared Owl N	SE	● ● ● ● ● ● ●	• • • • • • •
	SW	● ● ● ● ● ● ●	· · · · · · ·
	N	· · · · · · ·	· · · · · · ·

M = migrating species, N = nesting species

* = The Arizona Bird Committee desires documented sightings of this species to substantiate the species as an Arizona bird species.

· · · · · · · = Poor   • • • • • • • = Moderate   ● ● ● ● ● ● ● = Good

SPECIES   REGION   Seasonal Occurence and Abundance

✔   Winter   Summer

☐	Species	Region	Winter	Summer
	Short-eared Owl N	SE	• • • • • • • (Moderate)	
		SW	• • • • • • • (Moderate)	
		N		· · · · · · · (Poor)
	Northern Saw-whet Owl N	SE	· · · · · · · (Poor)	· · · · · · · (Poor)
		SW	· · · · · · · (Poor)	· · · · · · · (Poor)
		N	●●●●●●● (Good)	●●●●●●● (Good)
	Lesser Nighthawk N	SE	· · · · · · · (Poor)	●●●●●●● (Good)
		SW	· · · · · · · (Poor)	●●●●●●● (Good)
		N		· · · · · · · (Poor)
	Common Nighthawk N	SE		●●●●●●● (Good)
		SW	• • • • • • • (Moderate)	· · · · · · · (Poor)
		N		●●●●●●● (Good)
	Common Poorwill N	SE	· · · · · · · (Poor)	●●●●●●● (Good)
		SW		●●●●●●● (Good)
		N		●●●●●●● (Good)
	Buff-collared Nightjar M	SE		· · · · · · · (Poor)
	Whip-poor-will N	SE	· · · · · · · (Poor)	●●●●●●● (Good)
		SW	· · · · · · · (Poor)	· · · · · · · (Poor)
		N		· · · · · · · (Poor)
	Chimney Swift M	SE		· · · · · · · (Poor)
		SW	· · · · · · · (Poor)	· · · · · · · (Poor)
	Vaux's Swift M	SE	· · · · · · · (Poor)	· · · · · · · (Poor)
		SW	· · · · · · · (Poor)	· · · · · · · (Poor)
		N	· · · · · · · (Poor)	· · · · · · · (Poor)
	White-throated Swift N	SE	●●●●●●● (Good)	●●●●●●● (Good)
		SW	●●●●●●● (Good)	●●●●●●● (Good)
		N		●●●●●●● (Good)
	Broad-billed Hummingbird N	SE	· · · · · · · (Poor)	●●●●●●● (Good)
		SW	· · · · · · · (Poor)	
	White-eared Hummingbird* M	SE		· · · · · · · (Poor)

M = migrating species, N = nesting species

  * = The Arizona Bird Committee desires documented sightings of this species to substantiate the species as an Arizona bird species.

    · · · · · · · = Poor   • • • • • • • = Moderate   ●●●●●●● = Good

✔	SPECIES	REGION	Winter	Summer
☐	Berylline Hummingbird N	SE		· · · · · · · ·
☐	Violet-crowned Hummingbird N	SE	· · · · · · · ·	• • • • • • •
☐	Blue-throated Hummingbird N	SE	· · · · · · ·	● ● ● ● ● ● ●
☐	Magnificent Hummingbird N	SE N	· · · · · · ·	● ● ● ● ● ● ● • • • • • • •
☐	Plain-capped Starthroat* M	SE SW	· · · · · · · · · · · · · ·	· · · · · · · · · · · · · ·
☐	Lucifer Hummingbird* N	SE		· · · · · · ·
☐	Black-chinned Hummingbird N	SE N		● ●
☐	Anna's Hummingbird N	SE SW N	• • • • • • • • • • • • • •	· ·
☐	Costa's Hummingbird N	SE SW	· · · · · · · ● ● ● ● ● ● ●	● ● ● ● ● ● ● ● ● ● ● ● ● ●
☐	Calliope Hummingbird M	SE SW N	· · · · · · ·	· · · · · · · · · · · · · · • • • • • • •
☐	Broad-tailed Hummingbird N	SE SW N	· · · · · · ·	● ● ● ● ● ● ● ● ● ● ● ● ● ●
☐	Rufous Hummingbird M	SE SW N	· · · · · · ·	• •

M = migrating species,   N = nesting species
 * = The Arizona Bird Committee desires documented sightings of this species to substantiate the species as an Arizona bird species.

· · · · · · · · = Poor   • • • • • • • = Moderate   ● ● ● ● ● ● ● = Good

SPECIES	REGION	Winter	Summer
Allen's Hummingbird M	SE		·······
	SW		·······
Elegant Trogon N	SE	········	●●●●●●●
Eared Trogon* M	SE		·······
Belted Kingfisher N	SE	●●●●●●●	
	SW	●●●●●●●	
	N		•••••••
Green Kingfisher M	SE	········	·······
Lewis' Woodpecker N	SE	········	
	SW	········	
	N	●●●●●●●	●●●●●●●
Acorn Woodpecker N	SE	●●●●●●●	●●●●●●●
	SW	········	········
	N	●●●●●●●	●●●●●●●
Gila Woodpecker N	SE	●●●●●●●	●●●●●●●
	SW	●●●●●●●	●●●●●●●
		········	········
Yellow-bellied Sapsucker Red-naped N	SE	●●●●●●●	
	SW	●●●●●●●	
	N	●●●●●●●	●●●●●●●
Yellow-bellied Sapsucker Eastern M	SE	········	
	SW	········	
Red-breasted Sapsucker M	SE	········	
	SW	········	
	N	········	········
Williamson's Sapsucker N	SE	●●●●●●●	········
	SW	········	
	N	········	●●●●●●●

M = migrating species,   N = nesting species
* = The Arizona Bird Committee desires documented sightings of this species to substantiate the species as an Arizona bird species.
· · · · · · · · = Poor   • • • • • • • = Moderate   ●●●●●●● = Good

SPECIES   REGION   Seasonal Occurence and Abundance

✔ Species	Region	Winter	Summer
Ladder-backed Woodpecker N	SE	Moderate	Moderate
	SW	Moderate	Moderate
	N	Poor	Poor
Downy Woodpecker N	SE	Poor	
	SW	Poor	
	N	Moderate	Moderate
Hairy Woodpecker N	SE	Moderate	Moderate
	N	Moderate	Moderate
Strickland's Woodpecker N	SE	Moderate	Moderate
Three-toed Woodpecker N	N	Moderate	Moderate
Northern Flicker Yellow-shafted M	SE	Poor	
	SW	Poor	
	N	Poor	
Northern Flicker Red-shafted N	SE	Moderate	Moderate
	SW	Moderate	Moderate
	N	Moderate	Moderate
Northern Flicker Gilded N	SE	Moderate	Moderate
	SW	Moderate	Moderate
Northern Beardless-Tyrannulet N	SE	Moderate	Moderate
	SW	Poor	Poor
Olive-sided Flycatcher N	SE	Moderate	Poor
	SW	Moderate	Poor
	N		Moderate
Greater Pewee N	SE	Poor	Moderate
	SW	Poor	
	N		Poor
Western Wood-Pewee N	SE		Moderate
	SW	Moderate	Poor
	N		Moderate

M = migrating species, N = nesting species
* = The Arizona Bird Committee desires documented sightings of this species to substantiate the species as an Arizona bird species.
· · · · · · · = Poor   • • • • • • = Moderate   ● ● ● ● ● ● = Good

SPECIES   REGION   Seasonal Occurence and Abundance

✔	Species	Region	Winter	Summer
☐	Willow Flycatcher N	SE	Moderate	Moderate
		SW	Moderate	Moderate
		N	Moderate	Moderate
☐	Least Flycatcher* N		Poor	Poor
☐	Hammond's Flycatcher N	SE	Moderate	Moderate
		SW	Poor	Moderate
		N	Moderate	Poor
☐	Dusky Flycatcher N	SE	Moderate	Moderate
		SW	Poor	Moderate
		N		Good
☐	Gray Flycatcher N	SE	Good	
		SW	Good	
		N		Good
☐	Western Flycatcher N	SE	Poor	Good
		SW	Poor	Moderate
		N		Good
☐	Buff-breasted Flycatcher N	SE		Moderate
☐	Black Phoebe N	SE	Good	Good
		SW	Good	Moderate
		N	Poor	Moderate
☐	Eastern Phoebe M	SE	Poor	
		SW	Poor	
		N	Poor	Poor
☐	Say's Phoebe N	SE	Poor	Poor
		SW	Poor	Poor
		N	Moderate	Poor
☐	Vermilion Flycatcher N	SE	Good	Good
		SW	Good	Good
		N	Poor	Poor
☐	Dusky-capped Flycatcher N	SE		Good
		SW	Poor	Poor
		N	Poor	Poor

M = migrating species, N = nesting species
* = The Arizona Bird Committee desires documented sightings of this species to substantiate the species as an Arizona bird species.

· · · · · · · = Poor   • • • • • • • = Moderate   ●●●●●●● = Good

✔	SPECIES	REGION	Winter	Summer
☐	Ash-throated Flycatcher N	SE	· · · · · · ·	●●●●●●●
		SW	• • • • • • •	●●●●●●●
		N		●●●●●●●
☐	Brown-crowned Flycatcher N	SE		●●●●●●●
		SW		●●●●●●●
☐	Sulphur-bellied Flycatcher N	SE		●●●●●●●
☐	Tropical Kingbird N	SE	· · · · · · ·	· · · · · · ·
		SW		
☐	Cassin's Kingbird N	SE		●●●●●●●
		SW	• • • • • • •	· · · · · · ·
		N		●●●●●●●
☐	Thick-billed Kingbird N	SE	· · · · · · ·	· · · · · · ·
		SW		
☐	Western Kingbird N	SE		●●●●●●●
		SW		●●●●●●●
		N		●●●●●●●
☐	Eastern Kingbird M	SE	●●●●●●●	●●●●●●●
		SW	●●●●●●●	●●●●●●●
		N	●●●●●●●	●●●●●●●
☐	Scissor-tailed Flycatcher N	SE	●●●●●●●	●●●●●●●
		SW	●●●●●●●	●●●●●●●
		N	●●●●●●●	●●●●●●●
☐	Rose-throated Becard N	SE		· · · · · · ·
☐	Horned Lark N	SE	●●●●●●●	●●●●●●●
		SW	●●●●●●●	●●●●●●●
		N	●●●●●●●	●●●●●●●
☐	Purple Martin N	SE		●●●●●●●
		SW		· · · · · · ·
		N		●●●●●●●

M = migrating species,   N = nesting species
 * = The Arizona Bird Committee desires documented sightings of this species to substantiate the species as an Arizona bird species.

· · · · · · · = Poor   • • • • • • • = Moderate   ●●●●●●● = Good

SPECIES   REGION   Seasonal Occurrence and Abundance

✔ Species	Region	Winter	Summer
Tree Swallow N	SE	Poor	Moderate
	SW	Moderate	
	N	Poor	Poor
Violet-green Swallow N	SE		Good
	SW	Poor	Moderate
	N		Good
Northern Rough-winged Swallow N	SE	Poor	Good
	SW	Poor	Good
	N	Poor	Poor
Bank Swallow M	SE	Moderate	Poor
	SW	Poor	Poor
	N	Poor	Poor
Cliff Swallow N	SE		Good
	SW		Good
	N		Good
Cave Swallow* N	SE		Poor
Barn Swallow N	SE		Good
	SW	Poor	
	N		Good
Gray Jay N	N		Poor
Steller's Jay N	SE	Moderate	Good
	SW	Poor	
	N	Moderate	Good
Scrub Jay N	SE	Good	Good
	SW	Poor	
	N	Moderate	Good
Gray-breasted Jay N	SE	Good	Good
Pinyon Jay N	SE	Poor	
	SW	Poor	
	N	Good	Good

M = migrating species, N = nesting species

* = The Arizona Bird Committee desires documented sightings of this species to substantiate the species as an Arizona bird species.

· · · · · · · = Poor   • • • • • • = Moderate   ● ● ● ● ● ● = Good

SPECIES	REGION	Seasonal Occurrence and Abundance Winter	Summer
Clark's Nutcracker N	SE	Poor	
	SW	Poor	
	N	Good	Good
Black-billed Magpie N	N	Poor	Poor
American Crow N	SE	Poor	Poor
	SW	Moderate	
	N	Good	Good
Chihuahuan Raven N	SE	Moderate	Moderate
	SW	Poor	Poor
Common Raven N	SE	Moderate	Moderate
	SW	Moderate	Moderate
	N	Moderate	Moderate
Black-capped Chickadee* M	N	Poor	
Mexican Chickadee N	SE	Poor	Poor
Mountain Chickadee N	SE	Good	Good
	SW	Poor	
	N	Good	Good
Bridled Titmouse N	SE	Good	Good
	SW	Poor	
Plain Titmouse N	SE	Poor	Poor
	N	Good	Good
Verdin N	SE	Good	Good
	SW	Good	Good
Bushtit N	SE	Good	Good
	SW	Poor	Poor
	N	Good	Good

M = migrating species,   N = nesting species

 * = The Arizona Bird Committee desires documented sightings of this species to substantiate the species as an Arizona bird species.

. . . . = Poor   • • • • • • = Moderate   ● ● ● ● ● ● = Good

✔ Species	Region	Winter	Summer
Red-breasted Nuthatch N	SE	Good	Good
	SW	Poor	
	N	Good	Good
White-breasted Nuthatch N	SE	Good	Good
	SW	Poor	
	N	Good	Good
Pygmy Nuthatch N	SE	Good	Good
	SW	Poor	Poor
	N	Good	Good
Brown Creeper N	SE	Good	Good
	SW	Moderate	
	N	Good	Good
Cactus Wren N	SE	Good	Good
	SW	Good	Good
Rock Wren N	SE	Good	Good
	SW	Moderate	Moderate
	N	Good	Good
Canyon Wren N	SE	Good	Good
	SW	Good	Good
	N	Good	Good
Bewick's Wren N	SE	Good	Good
	SW	Good	Poor
	N	Poor	Good
House Wren N	SE	Good	Good
	SW	Good	
	N		Good
Winter Wren M	SE	Good	
	SW	Poor	
	N	Poor	
Marsh Wren N	SE	Good	
	SW	Good	Good
	N	Poor	Good
American Dipper N	SE	Poor	Poor
	SW	Poor	Poor
	N	Good	Good

M = migrating species,   N = nesting species

 * = The Arizona Bird Committee desires documented sightings of this species to substantiate the species as an Arizona bird species.

· · · · · · · · = Poor   • • • • • • • = Moderate   ● ● ● ● ● ● ● = Good

SPECIES ✔	REGION	Seasonal Occurence and Abundance	
		Winter	Summer
Golden-crowned Kinglet N	SE	Poor	Good
	SW	Poor	Good
	N	Good	Good
Ruby-crowned Kinglet N	SE	Good	Poor
	SW	Good	
	N	Poor	Good
Blue-gray Gnatcatcher N	SE	Good	Good
	SW	Good	Poor
	N		Good
Black-tailed Gnatcatcher N	SE	Good	Good
	SW	Good	Good
	N	Poor	Poor
Black-capped Gnatcatcher* N	SE		Poor
Eastern Bluebird N	SE	Good	Good
Western Bluebird N	SE	Good	Good
	SW	Good	
	N	Good	Good
Mountain Bluebird N	SE	Good	Poor
	SW	Good	
	N	Good	Good
Townsend's Solitaire N	SE	Good	Poor
	SW	Good	
	N	Good	Good
Veery* N	N		Poor
Swainson's Thrush N	SE	Poor	Poor
	SW	Poor	Poor
	N		Poor
Hermit Thrush N	SE	Good	Good
	SW	Good	
	N		Good

M = migrating species, N = nesting species
 * = The Arizona Bird Committee desires documented sightings of this species to substantiate
 the species as an Arizona bird species.
 · · · · · · · · = Poor   • • • • • • = Moderate   ● ● ● ● ● ● = Good

SPECIES | REGION | Seasonal Occurence and Abundance

✔			Winter	Summer
Wood Thrush* M		SE	· · · · · · · ·	· · · · · · · ·
		SW	· · · · · · · ·	· · · · · · · ·
		N	· · · · · · · ·	· · · · · · · ·
Rufous-backed Robin M		SE	· · · · · · · ·	· · · · · · · ·
		SW	· · · · · · · ·	· · · · · · · ·
		N	· · · · · · · ·	· · · · · · · ·
American Robin N		SE	● ● ● ● ● ● ●	● ● ● ● ● ● ● ●
		SW	● ● ● ● ● ● ●	· · · · · · · ·
		N	● ● ● ● ● ● ●	● ● ● ● ● ● ●
Varied Thrush M		SE	· · · · · · · ·	
		SW	· · · · · · · ·	
		N	· · · · · · · ·	
Aztec Thrush* M		SE		· · · · · · · ·
Gray Catbird N		SE	· · · · · · · ·	· · · · · · · ·
		SW	· · · · · · · ·	· · · · · · · ·
		N		● ● ● ● ● ● ●
Northern Mockingbird N		SE	● ● ● ● ● ● ●	● ● ● ● ● ● ●
		SW	● ● ● ● ● ● ●	● ● ● ● ● ● ●
		N	· · · · · · · ·	● ● ● ● ● ● ●
Sage Thrasher N		SE	● ● ● ● ● ● ●	· · · · · · · ·
		SW	● ● ● ● ● ● ●	
		N	● ● ● ● ● ● ●	● ● ● ● ● ● ●
Brown Thrasher M		SE	· · · · · · · ·	
		SW	· · · · · · · ·	
		N	· · · · · · · ·	· · · · · · · ·
Bendire's Thrasher N		SE	● ● ● ● ● ● ●	● ● ● ● ● ● ●
		SW	● ● ● ● ● ● ●	● ● ● ● ● ● ●
		N		● ● ● ● ● ● ●
Curve-billed Thrasher N		SE	● ● ● ● ● ● ●	● ● ● ● ● ● ●
		SW	● ● ● ● ● ● ●	● ● ● ● ● ● ●
Crissal Thrasher N		SE	● ● ● ● ● ● ●	● ● ● ● ● ● ●
		SW	● ● ● ● ● ● ●	● ● ● ● ● ● ●
		N	· · · · · · · ·	· · · · · · · ·

M = migrating species,   N = nesting species
 * = The Arizona Bird Committee desires documented sightings of this species to substantiate the species as an Arizona bird species.
· · · · · · · = Poor   ● ● ● ● ● ● ● = Moderate   ● ● ● ● ● ● ● = Good

SPECIES — REGION — Seasonal Occurence and Abundance

✔ Species	Region	Winter	Summer
Le Conte's Thrasher N	SE	Poor	Poor
	SW	Good	Good
Water Pipit N	SE	Moderate	
	SW	Moderate	
	N	Poor	Poor
Sprague's Pipit M	SE	Moderate	
	SW	Poor	
	N	Poor	Poor
Bohemian Waxwing M	SE	Poor	
	SW	Poor	
	N	Poor	
Cedar Waxwing M	SE	Moderate	
	SW	Moderate	
	N	Poor	Poor
Phainopepla N	SE	Moderate	Moderate
	SW	Moderate	Moderate
	N	Moderate	Poor
Northern Shrike M	SE	Poor	Poor
	SW	Poor	Poor
	N	Moderate	
Loggerhead Shrike N	SE	Moderate	Moderate
	SW	Moderate	Moderate
	N	Moderate	Moderate
European Starling N	SE	Moderate	Moderate
	SW	Moderate	Moderate
	N	Moderate	Moderate
Bell's Vireo N	SE		Moderate
	SW	Poor	Moderate
	N		Poor
Gray Vireo N	SE	Poor	Poor
	SW	Moderate	
	N		Moderate
Solitary Vireo *plumbeus* form N	SE	Poor	Moderate
	SW	Poor	Poor
	N		Moderate

M = migrating species,   N = nesting species

* = The Arizona Bird Committee desires documented sightings of this species to substantiate the species as an Arizona bird species.

· · · · · · · = Poor   • • • • • • = Moderate   ● ● ● ● ● ● ● = Good

SPECIES	REGION	Winter	Summer
Solitary Vireo *cassinii* form N	SE	······· (Poor)	••••••• (Moderate)
	SW	······· (Poor)	••••••• (Moderate)
	N	••••••• (Moderate)	••••••• (Moderate)
Yellow-throated Vireo M	SE	······· (Poor)	······· (Poor)
	SW	······· (Poor)	······· (Poor)
	N	······· (Poor)	······· (Poor)
Hutton's Vireo N	SE	●●●●●●● (Good)	●●●●●●● (Good)
	SW	······· (Poor)	
Warbling Vireo N	SE		●●●●●●● (Good)
	SW	••••••• (Moderate)	••••••• (Moderate)
	N		●●●●●●● (Good)
Philadelphia Vireo* M	SE	······· (Poor)	······· (Poor)
	SW	······· (Poor)	······· (Poor)
	N	······· (Poor)	······· (Poor)
Red-eyed Vireo M	SE	······· (Poor)	······· (Poor)
	SW	······· (Poor)	······· (Poor)
	N	······· (Poor)	······· (Poor)
Yellow-green Vireo M	SE	······· (Poor)	······· (Poor)
	SW	······· (Poor)	······· (Poor)
Golden-winged Warbler M	SW	······· (Poor)	······· (Poor)
	N	······· (Poor)	······· (Poor)
Tennessee Warbler M	SE	······· (Poor)	······· (Poor)
	SW	······· (Poor)	······· (Poor)
	N	······· (Poor)	······· (Poor)
Orange-crowned Warbler N	SE	●●●●●●● (Good)	······· (Poor)
	SW	●●●●●●● (Good)	
	N	••••••• (Moderate)	••••••• (Moderate)
Nashville Warbler M	SE	••••••• (Moderate)	••••••• (Moderate)
	SW	••••••• (Moderate)	••••••• (Moderate)
	N	••••••• (Moderate)	••••••• (Moderate)
Virginia's Warbler N	SE		······· (Poor)
	SW	······· (Poor)	●●●●●●● (Good)
	N		······· (Poor)

M = migrating species, N = nesting species

 * = The Arizona Bird Committee desires documented sightings of this species to substantiate the species as an Arizona bird species.

· · · · · · · = Poor   • • • • • • • = Moderate   ●●●●●●● = Good

SPECIES   REGION   Seasonal Occurence and Abundance

Species	Region	Winter	Summer
Lucy's Warbler N	SE		● ● ● ● ● ● ●
	SW		● ● ● ● ● ● ●
	N		• • • • • • •
Northern Parula M	SE	· · · · · · ·	· · · · · · ·
	SW	· · · · · · ·	· · · · · · ·
	N	· · · · · · ·	· · · · · · ·
Yellow Warbler N	SE	· · · · · · ·	● ● ● ● ● ● ●
	SW	· · · · · · ·	● ● ● ● ● ● ●
	N		● ● ● ● ● ● ●
Chestnut-sided Warbler M	SE	· · · · · · ·	· · · · · · ·
	SW	· · · · · · ·	· · · · · · ·
	N	· · · · · · ·	· · · · · · ·
Magnolia Warbler* M	SE	· · · · · · ·	· · · · · · ·
	SW	· · · · · · ·	· · · · · · ·
	N	· · · · · · ·	· · · · · · ·
Black-throated Blue Warbler M	SE	· · · · · · ·	· · · · · · ·
	SW	· · · · · · ·	· · · · · · ·
	N	· · · · · · ·	· · · · · · ·
Yellow-rumped Warbler Audubon's N	SE	● ● ● ● ● ●	● ● ● ● ● ● ●
	SW	● ● ● ● ● ●	● ● ● ● ● ● ●
	N	· · · · · · ·	● ● ● ● ● ● ●
Yellow-rumped Warbler Myrtle M	SE	· · · · · · ·	· · · · · · ·
	SW	· · · · · · ·	· · · · · · ·
	N	· · · · · · ·	· · · · · · ·
Black-throated Gray Warbler N	SE	· · · · · · ·	● ● ● ● ● ● ●
	SW	· · · · · · ·	• • • • • • •
	N		● ● ● ● ● ● ●
Townsend's Warbler M	SE	· · · · · · ·	• • • • • • •
	SW	· · · · · · ·	• • • • • • •
	N	• • • • • • •	• • • • • • •
Hermit Warbler M	SE	• • • • • • •	• • • • • • •
	SW	· · · · · · ·	• • • • • • •
	N	• • • • • • •	• • • • • • •
Black-throated Green Warbler* M	SE	· · · · · · ·	· · · · · · ·
	SW	· · · · · · ·	· · · · · · ·
	N	· · · · · · ·	· · · · · · ·

M = migrating species,   N = nesting species

* = The Arizona Bird Committee desires documented sightings of this species to substantiate the species as an Arizona bird species.

· · · · · · · = Poor   • • • • • • • = Moderate   ● ● ● ● ● ● ● = Good

SPECIES   REGION   Seasonal Occurence and Abundance

✔			Winter	Summer
☐	Blackburnian Warbler* M	SE SW N	· ·	· ·
☐	Yellow-throated Warbler M	SE SW N	· ·	· ·
☐	Grace's Warbler N	SE N		● ● ● ● ● ● ● ● ● ● ● ● ● ● ●
☐	Prairie Warbler* M	SE	· · · · · · · ·	· · · · · · · ·
☐	Palm Warbler* M	SE SW N	· ·	· ·
☐	Bay-breasted Warbler* M	SE SW N	· ·	· ·
☐	Blackpoll Warbler* M	SE SW N	· ·	· ·
☐	Black and White Warbler M	SE SW N	· ·	· ·
☐	American Redstart N	SE SW N	· ·	· · · · · · · · · · · · · · · · ● ● ● ● ● ● ●
☐	Prothonotary Warbler* M	SE SW N	· ·	· ·
☐	Worm-eating Warbler M	SE SW N	· ·	· ·
☐	Ovenbird M	SE SW N	· ·	· ·

M = migrating species, N = nesting species
  * = The Arizona Bird Committee desires documented sightings of this species to substantiate
  the species as an Arizona bird species.
    · · · · · · · · = Poor   ● ● ● ● ● ● = Moderate   ● ● ● ● ● ● = Good

SPECIES   REGION Seasonal Occurence and Abundance

✔ Species	Region	Winter	Summer
Northern Waterthrush M	SE	Moderate	Moderate
	SW	Moderate	Moderate
	N	Moderate	Moderate
Louisiana Waterthrush* M	SE	Poor	Poor
Kentucky Warbler* M	SE	Poor	Poor
	SW	Poor	Poor
	N	Poor	Poor
MacGillivray's Warbler N	SE	Moderate	Moderate
	SW	Moderate	Moderate
	N		Good
Common Yellowthroat N	SE	Moderate	Good
	SW	Good	Good
	N		Good
Hooded Warbler M	SE	Poor	Poor
	SW	Poor	Poor
	N	Poor	Poor
Wilson's Warbler M	SE	Poor	Moderate
	SW	Poor	Moderate
	N	Moderate	Moderate
Canada Warbler* M	SE	Poor	Poor
	SW	Poor	Poor
	N	Poor	Poor
Red-faced Warbler N	SE		Good
	SW	Poor	
	N		Good
Painted Redstart N	SE	Poor	Good
	SW	Poor	Poor
	N		Moderate
Yellow-breasted Chat N	SE		Good
	SW		Good
	N		Moderate
Olive Warbler N	SE	Good	Good
	N	Poor	Moderate

M = migrating species,   N = nesting species

* = The Arizona Bird Committee desires documented sightings of this species to substantiate the species as an Arizona bird species.

· · · · · · · · = Poor   • • • • • • = Moderate   ● ● ● ● ● ● = Good

✔ SPECIES	REGION	Winter	Summer
Hepatic Tanager N	SE	Poor	Good
	SW	Moderate	Poor
	N		Poor
Summer Tanager N	SE	Poor	Good
	SW	Poor	Good
	N	Poor	Poor
Scarlet Tanager* M	SE	Poor	Poor
	SW	Poor	Poor
	N	Poor	Poor
Western Tanager N	SE	Poor	Good
	SW	Poor	Moderate
	N		Good
Northern Cardinal M	SE	Good	Good
	SW	Good	Good
Pyrrhuloxia N	SE	Good	Good
	SW	Moderate	Moderate
Yellow Grosbeak* M	SE	Poor	Poor
Rose-breasted Grosbeak M	SE	Poor	Poor
	SW	Poor	Poor
	N	Poor	Poor
Black-headed Grosbeak N	SE	Poor	Good
	SW	Poor	Good
	N		Good
Blue Grosbeak N	SE	Poor	Good
	SW	Poor	Good
	N		Good
Lazuli Bunting N	SE	Poor	Poor
	SW	Poor	Poor
	N		Moderate
Indigo Bunting N	SE		Good
	SW		Moderate
	N		Moderate

M = migrating species,   N = nesting species

* = The Arizona Bird Committee desires documented sightings of this species to substantiate the species as an Arizona bird species.

· · · · · · · = Poor   • • • • • • • = Moderate   ● ● ● ● ● ● ● = Good

SPECIES REGION Seasonal Occurence and Abundance

✔

Species	Region	Winter	Summer
Varied Bunting N	SE		● ● ● ● ● ● ●
	SW	· · · · · · ·	· · · · · · ·
Painted Bunting* M	SE	· · · · · · ·	· · · · · · ·
	SW	· · · · · · ·	· · · · · · ·
	N	· · · · · · ·	· · · · · · ·
Dickcissel M	SE	· · · · · · ·	· · · · · · ·
	SW	· · · · · · ·	· · · · · · ·
	N	· · · · · · ·	· · · · · · ·
Green-tailed Towhee N	SE	● ● ● ● ● ● ●	
	SW	● ● ● ● ● ● ●	
	N		● ● ● ● ● ● ●
Rufous-sided Towhee N	SE	● ● ● ● ● ● ●	● ● ● ● ● ● ●
	SW	● ● ● ● ● ● ●	
	N	· · · · · · ·	● ● ● ● ● ● ●
Brown Towhee N	SE	● ● ● ● ● ● ●	● ● ● ● ● ● ●
	SW	● ● ● ● ● ● ●	● ● ● ● ● ● ●
	N	· · · · · · ·	· · · · · · ·
Abert's Towhee N	SE	● ● ● ● ● ● ●	● ● ● ● ● ● ●
	SW	● ● ● ● ● ● ●	● ● ● ● ● ● ●
Botteri's Sparrow N	SE		● ● ● ● ● ● ●
Cassin's Sparrow N	SE	· · · · · · ·	● ● ● ● ● ● ●
	SW		· · · · · · ·
Rufous-winged Sparrow N	SE	● ● ● ● ● ● ●	● ● ● ● ● ● ●
Rufous-crowned Sparrow N	SE	● ● ● ● ● ● ●	● ● ● ● ● ● ●
	SW	● ● ● ● ● ● ●	● ● ● ● ● ● ●
	N	· · · · · · ·	· · · · · · ·
American Tree Sparrow M	SE	· · · · · · ·	· · · · · · ·
	SW	· · · · · · ·	· · · · · · ·
	N	· · · · · · ·	· · · · · · ·

M = migrating species,   N = nesting species

* = The Arizona Bird Committee desires documented sightings of this species to substantiate the species as an Arizona bird species.

· · · · · · · = Poor   ● ● ● ● ● ● ● = Moderate   ● ● ● ● ● ● ● = Good

✔	Species	Region	Winter	Summer
☐	Chipping Sparrow N	SE	Good	Poor
		SW	Good	
		N	Poor	Good
☐	Clay-colored Sparrow* M	SE	Poor	Poor
		SW	Poor	Poor
		N	Poor	Poor
☐	Brewer's Sparrow N	SE	Good	
		SW	Good	
		N		Good
☐	Black-chinned Sparrow N	SE	Good	Good
		SW	Poor	
		N		Poor
☐	Vesper Sparrow N	SE	Good	
		SW	Good	
		N		Good
☐	Lark Sparrow N	SE	Good	Good
		SW	Good	Poor
		N		Good
☐	Black-throated Sparrow N	SE	Good	Good
		SW	Good	Good
		N		Good
☐	Sage Sparrow N	SE	Good	
		SW	Good	
		N		Good
☐	Five-striped Sparrow N	SE	Poor	Poor
☐	Lark Bunting N	SE	Good	
		SW	Good	
		N	Poor	Poor
☐	Savannah Sparrow N	SE	Good	
		SW	Good	
		N	Poor	Poor
☐	Baird's Sparrow M	SE	Good	
		N	Poor	Poor

M = migrating species, N = nesting species

 * = The Arizona Bird Committee desires documented sightings of this species to substantiate the species as an Arizona bird species.

· · · · · · · = Poor   • • • • • • • = Moderate   ● ● ● ● ● ● ● = Good

SPECIES	REGION	Winter	Summer
Grasshopper Sparrow N	SE	Good	Good
	SW	Poor	Poor
	N	Poor	Poor
Fox Sparrow M	SE	Poor	
	SW		
	N	Poor	
Song Sparrow N	SE	Good	Good
	SW	Good	Good
	N	Good	Good
Lincoln's Sparrow N	SE	Good	
	SW	Good	
	N	Poor	Moderate
Swamp Sparrow M	SE	Poor	
	SW	Good	
	N	Poor	
White-throated Sparrow N	SE	Good	
	SW	Poor	
	N	Poor	
Golden-crowned Sparrow M	SE	Poor	
	SW	Poor	
	N	Poor	Poor
White-crowned Sparrow N	SE	Good	Poor
	SW	Good	Poor
	N	Good	Moderate
Harris' Sparrow M	SE	Poor	
	SW	Poor	
	N	Poor	
Dark-eyed Junco White-winged M	N	Poor	
Dark-eyed Junco Slate-colored M	SE	Poor	
	SW	Poor	
	N	Poor	
Dark-eyed Junco Oregon form M	SE	Good	
	SW	Good	
	N	Good	

Seasonal Occurence and Abundance

M = migrating species, N = nesting species

* = The Arizona Bird Committee desires documented sightings of this species to substantiate the species as an Arizona bird species.

· · · · · · · = Poor   ● ● ● ● ● ● = Moderate   ● ● ● ● ● ● ● = Good

✔ SPECIES	REGION	Winter	Summer
Dark-eyed Junco Gray-headed *canceps* N	SE	Moderate	
	SW	Poor	
	N	Moderate	Poor
Dark-eyed Junco Gray-headed *drosalis* N	SE	Poor	
	N	Moderate	Good
Yellow-eyed Junco N	SE	Moderate	Good
McCown's Longspur M	SE	Moderate	
	SW	Poor	
	N	Poor	Poor
Lapland Longspur M	SW	Poor	
	N	Poor	
Chestnut-colored Longspur M	SE	Moderate	
	SW	Poor	
	N	Moderate	
Bobolink N	SE	Poor	Poor
	SW	Poor	Poor
	N		Poor
Red-winged Blackbird N	SE	Good	Good
	SW	Good	Good
	N	Good	Good
Eastern Meadowlark N	SE	Good	Good
	SW	Good	
	N		Good
Western Meadowlark N	SE	Good	Moderate
	SW	Good	Good
	N	Good	Good
Yellow-headed Blackbird N	SE	Moderate	Moderate
	SW	Moderate	Good
	N		Good
Rusty Blackbird* M	SE	Poor	
	SW	Poor	

M = migrating species, N = nesting species
* = The Arizona Bird Committee desires documented sightings of this species to substantiate the species as an Arizona bird species.

· · · · · · · = Poor   • • • • • • • = Moderate   ● ● ● ● ● ● ● = Good

✔	SPECIES	REGION	Winter	Summer
☐	Brewer's Blackbird N	SE	Moderate	
		SW	Moderate	
		N	Moderate	Moderate
☐	Great-tailed Grackle N	SE	Moderate	Moderate
		SW	Moderate	Moderate
		N	Poor	Poor
☐	Bronzed Cowbird N	SE	Moderate	Moderate
		SW	Moderate	Moderate
		N		
☐	Brown-headed Cowbird N	SE	Moderate	Moderate
		SW	Moderate	Moderate
		N		Good
☐	Orchard Oriole* M	SE	Poor	Poor
		SW	Poor	Poor
☐	Hooded Oriole N	SE	Poor	Good
		SW		Good
		N		Moderate
☐	Streak-backed Oriole* M	SE	Poor	Poor
☐	Northern Oriole 　　Bullock's form N	SE	Poor	Good
		SW	Poor	Good
		N		Good
☐	Northern Oriole 　　Baltimore form M	SE	Poor	Poor
		SW	Poor	Poor
		N	Poor	Poor
☐	Scott's Oriole N	SE	Poor	Good
		SW	Poor	Good
		N		Moderate
☐	Rosy Finch* 　　Gray-crowned M	N	Poor	
	Black M	N	Poor	
☐	Pine Grosbeak N	SE	Poor	Poor
		N	Moderate	Moderate

M = migrating species, N = nesting species
* = The Arizona Bird Committee desires documented sightings of this species to substantiate the species as an Arizona bird species.

· · · · · · · · = Poor   • • • • • • • = Moderate   ● ● ● ● ● ● ● = Good

✔ Species	Region	Winter	Summer
Purple Finch N	SE	Poor	
	SW	Poor	
	N	Poor	Poor
Cassin's Finch N	SE	Poor	
	SW	Poor	
	N	Good	Good
House Finch N	SE	Good	Good
	SW	Good	Good
	N	Good	Good
Red Crossbill N	SE	Good	Good
	SW	Poor	
	N	Good	Good
Pine Siskin N	SE	Good	Good
	SW	Poor	
	N	Good	Good
Lesser Goldfinch N	SE	Good	Good
	SW	Good	Good
	N	Good	Good
Lawrence's Goldfinch N	SE	Poor	
	SW	Poor	Poor
American Goldfinch M	SE	Good	
	SW	Good	
	N	Good	
Evening Grosbeak N	SE	Poor	Poor
	SW	Poor	
	N	Good	Good
House Sparrow N		Good	Good
		Good	Good
		Good	Good

M = migrating species,   N = nesting species
 * = The Arizona Bird Committee desires documented sightings of this species to substantiate the species as an Arizona bird species.

· · · · · · · · = Poor   • • • • • • = Moderate   ● ● ● ● ● ● ● = Good

CHAPTER 5

Arizona bird specialties

Arizona has so many "specialties" that it is difficult to decide just what species are most representative of the region. The Buff-collared Nightjar is seen nowhere else in the nation, as is the Elegant Trogon. The Greater Road-runner is almost synonymous with the state, and the Montezuma Quail is also the object of many quests as birders head to Arizona for rare birds.

This list could easily have included 200 birds, but I pared it down to only 127, most of which are closely identified with the region by birders from around the world.

A distribution map showing the general distribution in the state, a habitat preference, your chances of seeing the bird (Poor, Moderate, or Good), and some key sites to look for it are all included for each specialty.

Eared Grebe

W

Habits: Winters in open lakes and reservoirs. Migrates north for breeding.

Chances: Good.

Key Sites: Any of the national wildlife refuges along the Lower Colorado River, such as Havasu and Imperial.

Mexican Duck

Y

Habits: Rare year-round resident of ponds and marshes of southeastern Arizona.

Chances: Poor.

Key Sites: San Simon Marsh and along the San Pedro River.

Redhead

B

Habits: Freshwater marshes.

Chances: Poor to Moderate.

Key Sites: Breeding colonies along the Lower Colorado River in wildlife refuges, and on marshes of White Mountains. Jacques Marsh is one of these locations.

Greater Scaup

W

Habits: Winters in lakes along the Lower Colorado River.

Chances: Moderate to Good.

Key Sites: Mittry and Martinez lakes, Lake Havasu, and Topock Marsh.

 = Winter   = Year-round   = Breeding (Summer)

Black Rail

Y

Habits: Lives in grassy marshes and feeds in stubble fields.

Chances: Poor.

Key Sites: Mittry Lake and Betty's Kitchen south along Lower Colorado River to Mexican border.

Clapper Rail—Yuma Subspecies

Y

Habits: Brackish marshes along the Lower Colorado River.

Chances: Poor.

Key Sites: Marshes along the Lower Colorado River and nearby lakes.

Mountain Plover

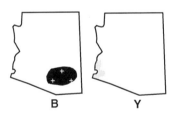

B   Y

Habits: Arid and semi-arid plains and grasslands.

Chances: Moderate.

Key Sites: Along the farmlands on the Arizona side of the Lower Colorado River inland along Interstate 8.

Greater Yellowlegs

W

Habits: Winters in open marshes, mudflats, ponds, and streams.

Chances: Moderate.

Key Sites: Marshes and ponds along the Lower Colorado River and near ponds along the southern portion of the state and in New Mexico.

 = Winter   = Year-round   = Breeding (Summer)

Chukar

Y

Habits:	Arid mountains and canyons.
Chances:	Moderate.
Key Sites:	Around Mount Trumbull and in open grasslands of the plateau.

Blue Grouse

Y

Habits:	Mixed forests in mountains.
Chances:	Poor
Key Sites:	Mount Trumbull area and in the Chuska Mountains in the Four Corners area.

Montezuma Quail

Y

Habits:	Mixed oak canyons with grassland/ mountain slopes with bunch grass.
Chances:	Poor.
Key Sites:	Buenos Aires National Wildlife Refuge, eastern portion of the White Mountains, and most of the small mountain ranges in the Sky Islands.

Masked Bobwhite

Y

Habits:	Grasslands and open brushlands.
Chances:	Poor.
Key Sites:	Buenos Aires National Wildlife Refuge is the only known site in the United States.

 = Winter   = Year-round   = Breeding (Summer)

Scaled Quail

Y

Habits:	Arid grasslands and brush.
Chances:	Poor to Moderate.
Key Sites:	Buenos Aires National Wildlife Refuge and grasslands around the Sky Islands.

Gambel's Quail

Y

Habits:	Chaparral, open grasslands, mixed oak grasslands.
Chances:	Good.
Key Sites:	Found throughout Arizona except in the northeastern corner.

Black Vulture

Y

Habits:	Seen soaring above all types of vegetation but is seldom seen in high mountains.
Chances:	Poor.
Key Sites:	An uncommon resident across southern Arizona. Santa Cruz Valley is a prime site, and it has nested on Picacho Peak.

Mississippi Kite

B

Habits:	Wooded canyon streams.
Chances:	Poor.
Key Sites:	Seen along the San Pedro River, near Dudleyville, and in Aravaipa Canyon.

 = Winter   = Year-round   = Breeding (Summer)

Swainson's Hawk

B

Habits: Summer resident of grasslands, and in sparse trees.

Chances: Good.

Key Sites: Many locations, but common around Tombstone, Douglas, Sonoita, and Sierra Vista.

Common Black-Hawk

B

Habits: Summer resident of riparian woodlands in low lands.

Chances: Poor.

Key Sites: More common in central Arizona, but seldom nests in the southern part of the state. Has been seen nesting in Aravaipa Canyon recently.

Gray Hawk

B

Habits: Summer resident of riparian woodlands of lowlands.

Chances: Moderate.

Key Sites: Along Santa Cruz and San Pedro rivers, Empire/Cienega Resource Conservation Area, and near Arivaca Creek.

Harris' Hawk

Y

Habits: Permanent resident of riparian woodlands, cactus, and mesquite brush.

Chances: Moderate.

Key Sites: Seen to the south and west of Tucson, and along Arizona Route 89 north of Tucson.

 = Winter   = Year-round   = Breeding (Summer)

Zone-tailed Hawk

B

Habits:	Summer resident of live-oak and pinyon forests. Forages over grasslands of lower mountain slopes.
Chances:	Poor to Moderate.
Key Sites:	Near any of the Sky Islands. Nesting sites are secret because of increased pressures from birders, photographers, and falconers.

Ferruginous Hawk

W   **Y**

Habits:	Winter resident of grasslands and deserts.
Chances:	Poor.
Key Sites:	Buenos Aires National Wildlife Refuge and along the Colorado Plateau.

Crested Caracara

Y

Habits:	Sonoran Desert.
Chances:	Poor.
Key Sites:	Landfill at Sells is the most dependable site. Also seen along the San Pedro River.

Prairie Falcon

Y

Habits:	Cliffs near open grasslands.
Chances:	Poor to Moderate.
Key Sites:	Has nested for years in the Chiricahua National Monument, but other nesting sites are kept secret for fear of falconers.

 = Winter   = Year-round   = Breeding (Summer)

Flammulated Owl

B

Habits:	Summer resident of pine and fir forests and higher-elevation oak woodlands.
Chances:	Poor.
Key Sites:	Upper end of Madera Canyon, upper end of Miller Canyon, South Fork Trail in Chiricahua Mountains, and Hualapai Mountain Park near Kingman.

Elf Owl

B

Habits:	Summer resident of saguaro cactus, sycamore trees, and telephone poles.
Chances:	Good.
Key Sites:	Saguaro National Monument, Organ Pipe Cactus National Monument, Sabino Canyon, and Madera Canyon.

Spotted Owl

Y

Habits:	Permanent resident of coniferous forests and cool, thickly wooded canyons.
Chances:	Poor.
Key Sites:	San Francisco Peaks area, Scheelite Canyon, upper Miller Canyon, and the Spotted Owl Trail near South Fork.

Band-tailed Pigeon

B   Y

Habits:	Permanent resident of oak canyons in mountains, as well as chaparral country.
Chances:	Good.
Key Sites:	Sonoita Creek Sanctuary near Patagonia.

 = Winter   = Year-round   = Breeding (Summer)

White-winged Dove

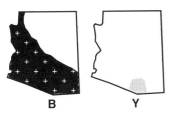

B   Y

Habits:	Summer resident of desert and lower oak woodlands.
Chances:	Good.
Key Sites:	Saguaro National Monument, Organ Pipe Cactus National Monument, Guadalupe Canyon, and Cave Creek Canyon.

Common Ground-Dove

Y

Habits:	River valleys at lower elevations.
Chances:	Good.
Key Sites:	Along Santa Cruz, San Pedro, and San Simon rivers.

Inca Dove

Habits:	Town and city parks.
Chances:	Good.
Key Sites:	Tucson city parks.

Yellow-billed Cuckoo

Y

Habits:	Summer resident of riparian woodlands.
Chances:	Poor.
Key Sites:	Along San Pedro River and at Patagonia Sonoita Creek Preserve.

 = Winter   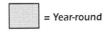 = Year-round   = Breeding (Summer)

Greater Roadrunner

Y

Habits: Permanent resident of deserts, brushlands, and brushy grasslands below 4,000 feet.

Chances: Good.

Key Sites: Saguaro National Monument, Organ Pipe Cactus National Monument, and Kofa National Wildlife Refuge are just a few sites out of many.

Lesser Nighthawk

B

Habits: Summer resident of low desert near lakes, towns, and irrigated land at dusk.

Chances: Good.

Key Sites: All across the southern portion of the state during summer.

Common Nighthawk

B

Habits: Feeds high in the air above grasslands at higher elevations near the mountains.

Chances: Good.

Key Sites: Along the higher grasslands around the Sky Islands, and in the White Mountains.

Whip-poor-will

B

Habits: Summer resident of thickly wooded mountainous areas. Feeds among low trees and roosts on lower limbs.

Chances: Moderate to Good.

Key Sites: Any of the wooded canyons of the Sky Islands such as Madera, Miller, and Cave Creek.

 = Winter   = Year-round   = Breeding (Summer)

Buff-collared Nightjar

Y

Habits:	Lives in juniper-mesquite brush and oak woodlands.
Chances:	Poor.
Key Sites:	First seen in U.S. in Guadalupe Canyon, but has been seen in Aravaipa and Madera canyons.

White-throated Swift

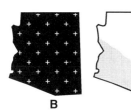

B   Y

Habits:	Permanent resident of cliffs at all elevations.
Chances:	Good.
Key Sites:	Upper Carr Canyon, Montezuma Pass in Coronado National Memorial, and along the Mogollon Rim.

Black-chinned Hummingbird

B

Habits:	Summer resident of desert and lower mountain slopes near water. Most common hummingbird of Southeastern Arizona.
Chances:	Good.
Key Sites:	Santa Rita Lodge, Southwestern Research Station in Chiricahua Mountains, Arizona-Sonora Desert Museum, and Ramsey Canyon.

Anna's Hummingbird

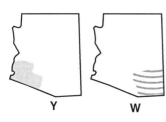

Y   W

Habits:	Fall migrant throughout southern Arizona to Chiricahua Mountains. Now nesting in January and February.
Chances:	Good.
Key Sites:	Feeders in the Phoenix and Tucson areas, and in the Catalina Mountains.

 = Winter   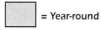 = Year-round   = Breeding (Summer)

Costa's Hummingbird

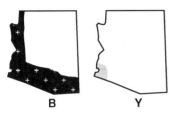

B   **Y**

Habits:	Winter and nesting resident in the low desert.
Chances:	Moderate to Good.
Key Sites:	Sabino Canyon, Tucson Mountain Park, Saguaro National Monument, and Florida Canyon.

Broad-tailed Hummingbird

B

Habits:	Summer resident of coniferous forests of higher mountains.
Chances:	Good.
Key Sites:	Meadows at Rustler Park during iris bloom, at feeders in Ramsey, Cave Creek, and Madera canyons, and at the Southwestern Research Station in the Chiricahua Mountains.

Lucifer Hummingbird

B

Habits:	Summer resident of lower mountain slopes.
Chances:	Poor.
Key Sites:	Feeders at Santa Rita Lodge, Cave Creek Canyon, and Coronado National Memorial.

Magnificent Hummingbird

B

Habits:	Summer resident of riparian woodlands in high mountains.
Chances:	Good.
Key Sites:	At feeders in Madera, Cave Creek, and Ramsey canyons, and at Patagonia Sonoita Creek Preserve in winter.

 = Winter   = Year-round   = Breeding (Summer)

Elegant Trogon

B

Habits:	Summer resident of canyons in Sky Islands, most notably Madera and Cave Creek canyons.
Chances:	Moderate.
Key Sites:	At upper end of Cave Creek Canyon along South Fork Trail and along Mount Wrightson Trail in upper Madera Canyon.

Green Kingfisher

W

Habits:	Winter resident in riparian growth along streams and ponds.
Chances:	Poor.
Key Sites:	Empire/Cienega Resource Conservation Area and San Pedro River.

Lewis' Woodpecker

Y

Habits:	Scattered and logged forests, along rivers, and in burned areas.
Chances:	Moderate.
Key Sites:	White Mountains.

Gila Woodpecker

Y

Habits:	Desert washes, saguaros, cottonwood groves, and in towns and cities.
Chances:	Good.
Key Sites:	Saguaro National Monument, Organ Pipe Cactus National Monument, Tucson, Phoenix, and in low desert across the southern portion of the state.

 = Winter   = Year-round   = Breeding (Summer)

Williamson's Sapsucker

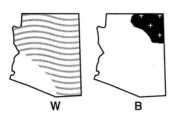

W   B

Habits: Migrant and winter resident of ponderosa pine forests.

Chances: Poor.

Key Sites: Most common in Chiricahua Mountains in April, but have been seen in the White Mountain region.

Ladder-backed Woodpecker

Y

Habits: Permanent resident of arid areas from brush lands and cactus of low deserts to riparian and oak woodlands.

Chances: Good.

Key Sites: Lower parts of mountain canyons, Saguaro National Monument, and Tucson Mountain Park.

Three-toed Woodpecker

Y

Habits: Permanent resident of conifer forests of northern Arizona.

Chances: Moderate.

Key Sites: White Mountains, San Francisco Peaks, and North Rim of the Grand Canyon.

Rose-throated Becard

Y

Habits: Summer resident of sycamore forests.

Chances: Poor.

Key Sites: Guadalupe Canyon, Patagonia Sonoita Creek Preserve, and Patagonia Lake.

 = Winter   = Year-round   = Breeding (Summer)

Cassin's Kingbird

B

Habits:	Summer resident of riparian woodlands, particularly in mountain canyons.
Chances:	Good.
Key Sites:	Any of the canyons of the Sky Islands such as Cave Creek, Madera, and Miller Canyons. Also at Patagonia Sonoita Creek Preserve.

Thick-billed Kingbird

B

Habits:	Summer resident of riparian woodlands at lower elevations. Nests in sycamores and cottonwoods.
Chances:	Poor.
Key Sites:	Best spot is Guadalupe Canyon, but has also been seen at Patagonia Sonoita Creek Preserve and Madera Canyon.

Sulphur-bellied Flycatcher

B

Habits:	Summer resident of mountain canyons, primarily in sycamores.
Chances:	Moderate in midsummer.
Key Sites:	Gardner and Madera canyons in Santa Rita Mountains, Ramsey, Miller, and Carr canyons in Huachucas, and Pinery Canyon in Chiricahuas.

Ash-throated Flycatcher

B   **Y**

Habits:	Summer resident of lower slopes and desert floor. Common in brushlands and open, arid woodlands.
Chances:	Good.
Key Sites:	Anywhere on lower slopes of Sky Islands and nearby desert.

 = Winter   = Year-round   = Breeding (Summer)

Dusky-capped Flycatcher

B

Habits:	Summer resident of live-oak forests of Sky Islands, primarily in canyons.
Chances:	Good.
Key Sites:	Seen in Patagonia Sonoita Creek in addition to mountain canyons.

Black Phoebe

W + Y   **B**

Habits:	Permanent resident near water at lower elevations.
Chances:	Good.
Key Sites:	In Sabino Canyon, any of the bridges across the Santa Cruz River, and along the San Pedro River. Also found at year-round marshes and lakes.

Say's Phoebe

B   **Y**

Habits:	Permanent resident from desert to lower slopes of mountains. Nests in rocky canyons and on cliffs.
Chances:	Good.
Key Sites:	Abundant in many areas, and has nested under eves of buildings at Southwestern Research Station in the Chiricahua Mountains.

Vermilion Flycatcher

Y

Habits:	Permanent resident near water. Likes mesquite, willow, and cottonwood.
Chances:	Good.
Key Sites:	Along the Santa Cruz River, but more are seen at Patagonia Sonoita Creek Preserve in summer than anywhere else in the United States.

 = Winter   = Year-round   = Breeding (Summer)

Northern Beardless-Tyrannulet

B

Habits: Summer resident near water. Likes mesquite, willow, and cottonwoods in the lower elevations.

Chances: Poor.

Key Sites: San Pedro and Santa Cruz rivers, and Patagonia Sonoita Creek Preserve.

Tree Swallow

W

B

Habits: Open country near water and marshes. Roosts in reeds around the water.

Chances: Good.

Key Sites: Along the Lower Colorado River in winter, and breeds in the Four Corners region.

Gray Jay

Y

Habits: Spruce and fir forests, and becomes tame around campgrounds and resorts.

Chances: Moderate.

Key Sites: Local year-round in southern portion of White Mountains and parts of the Chiricahua Mountains.

Steller's Jay

Y

Habits: Permanent resident of coniferous forests.

Chances: Good.

Key Sites: Around both North and South rims of the Grand Canyon, in the San Francisco Peaks area, higher locations in the White Mountains, on Mounts Graham and Lemmon, and at Rustler Park.

 = Winter   = Year-round   = Breeding (Summer)

Gray-breasted Jay

Y

Habits: Permanent resident of the live-oak belt of the Sky Islands. Also found northward to the Mogollon Rim. Travels in flocks of a dozen to fifty birds.

Chances: Good.

Key Sites: Any of the Sky Island canyons.

Pinyon Jay

Y

Habits: Permanent resident of pinyon-juniper forests and ranges into sagebrush country.

Chances: Good.

Key Sites: Any pinyon-juniper forests, particularly on the plateaus of northern Arizona.

Clark's Nutcracker

Y

Habits: Permanent resident of high mountains near the treeline. Common at resorts and campgrounds.

Chances: Moderate.

Key Sites: Best seen in the high mountains of the northeastern portion of the state.

American Crow

Y

Habits: Likes to be near people, but also found in woodlands and near farm fields.

Chances: Moderate.

Key Sites: Found near town dumps and farms in White Mountains and Four Corners area.

 = Winter   = Year-round   = Breeding (Summer)

Chihuahuan Raven

Y

Habits: Permanent resident of grasslands on high plains east of the Santa Rita Mountains.

Chances: Moderate to Good.

Key Sites: Look on top of tall yucca, windmills, and telephone poles east of Sonoita, in the San Pedro Valley, and the Sulphur Valley between Bisbee and Douglas.

Mexican Chickadee

Y

Habits: Permanent resident of the coniferous forests of the Chiricahua Mountains.

Chances: Poor to Moderate.

Key Sites: Pinery Canyon and Rustler Park.

Mountain Chickadee

Y

Habits: Permanent resident of coniferous forests north of Tucson.

Chances: Good.

Key Sites: Catalina and Pinaleño mountains, particularly along Mount Lemmon Road above Bear Canyon.

Bridled Titmouse

Y

Habits: Permanent resident of oak woodlands of all the Sky Islands.

Chances: Good.

Key Sites: Madera Canyon, Patagonia Sonoita Creek Preserve, Cave Creek Canyon, and all the Huachucas.

 = Winter   = Year-round   = Breeding (Summer)

Verdin

Y

Habits: Permanent resident of mesquite thickets and thorny brushlands at lower elevations.

Chances: Good.

Key Sites: Tucson Mountain Park, Sabino Canyon, Saguaro National Monument, and Florida Wash.

Cactus Wren

Y

Habits: Permanent resident of cactus and thorny brushlands of the lower elevations.

Chances: Good.

Key Sites: Organ Pipe Cactus National Monument, Saguaro National Monument, Tucson Mountain Park, Sabino Canyon, and all cactus patches in the low desert.

Canyon Wren

Y

Habits: Permanent resident of rocky canyons and cliffs near water at lower elevations.

Chances: Good.

Key Sites: Sycamore Canyon, Four Corners area, Hualapai Peak, oases at Organ Pipe Cactus National Monument, and Oak Creek Canyon.

Bewick's Wren

W Y

Habits: Permanent resident of brushlands, oak, riparian, and pinyon-juniper woodlands of mountain slopes throughout the state.

Chances: Good.

Key Sites: All over the state.

 = Winter   = Year-round   = Breeding (Summer)

Winter Wren

W

Habits: Winters in woodland underbrush of mountain slopes and summers in coniferous forests.

Chances: Good.

Key Sites: Forests around both rims of the Grand Canyon, White Mountains, and Sky Islands.

Black-tailed Gnatcatcher

Y

Habits: Permanent resident of desert brushlands.

Chances: Poor to Moderate.

Key Sites: Arizona-Sonora Desert Museum, cactus patch near Florida Wash, Organ Pipe Cactus National Monument, and locally in the Chihuahuan Desert east of the Sky Islands.

Eastern Bluebird

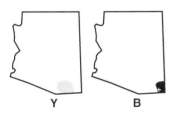

Y   B

Habits: Summer resident of pine and pine-oak woodlands of the Sky Islands.

Chances: Moderate.

Key Sites: Rustler Park, Reef Road in the Huachucas, and the Mount Wrightson Trail.

Western Bluebird

W   Y

Habits: Summer resident of the ponderosa forests of the higher mountains.

Chances: Moderate.

Key Sites: White Mountains, San Francisco Peaks area, north and south rims of the Grand Canyon, and the Sky Islands.

 = Winter   = Year-round   = Breeding (Summer)

Mountain Bluebird

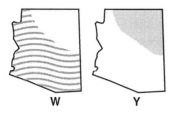

W Y

Habits: Winter: lower elevations. Year-round: higher elevations.

Chances: Moderate to Good.

Key Sites: Winter—near fields and orchards of the Santa Cruz, San Simon and San Pedro river valleys; meadows and brush of White Mountains; high plateaus south of the Grand Canyon.

Veery

Y

Habits: Damp deciduous woodlands.

Chances: Poor.

Key Sites: Local sites in the White Mountains. Check with local birders.

Sage Thrasher

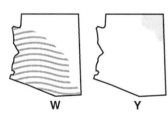

W Y

Habits: Winter resident in sparse vegetation of lower elevations. Breeds in the sagebrush country of the Four Corners area.

Chances: Moderate.

Key Sites: In the north during breeding. In winter, the plains east of the Chiricahuas, Sulphur Valley, and the lower San Pedro River.

Bendire's Thrasher

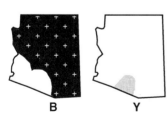

B Y

Habits: Year-round resident of desert cactus patches and thorny brush areas at the lower elevations.

Chances: Poor to Moderate.

Key Sites: San Xavier del Bac Mission south of Tucson, around the Arizona-Sonora Desert Museum, and the lower San Pedro Valley.

 = Winter   = Year-round   = Breeding (Summer)

Curve-billed Thrasher

Y

Habits: Permanent resident of cactus patches and thorny brush areas.

Chances: Good.

Key Sites: Guadalupe Canyon, Tucson Mountain Park, Sabino Canyon, between Tombstone and Douglas, and along the San Pedro and Santa Cruz rivers.

Crissal Thrasher

Y

Habits: Permanent resident of dense riparian thickets along waterways at lower elevations.

Chances: Moderate.

Key Sites: Florida Wash, along the Santa Cruz, Salt, and San Pedro rivers, the Lower Colorado River, Organ Pipe National Monument.

Le Conte's Thrasher

Y

Habits: Creosote brushlands of the southern part of the state.

Chances: Poor.

Key Sites: Organ Pipe Cactus National Monument, around Picacho Peak, and brushlands between Phoenix and Tucson.

Phainopepla

Y

B

Habits: Permanent resident of the brushlands of the desert and lower mountain slopes.

Chances: Good.

Key Sites: Florida Wash, Saguaro National Monument, Organ Pipe Cactus National Monument, and Sabino Canyon.

 = Winter   = Year-round   = Breeding (Summer)

173

Bell's Vireo

B   Y

Habits:	Breeds in riparian willow thickets along streams in southern part of the state, and along streams in Central Mountains.
Chances:	Moderate.
Key Sites:	Along the San Pedro, Lower Colorado, Santa Cruz, and Salt rivers and their tributaries.

Gray Vireo

W   B

Habits:	Arid, brushy hillsides, particularly in pinyon-juniper belt.
Chances:	Poor.
Key Sites:	Along the Mogollon Rim, Santa Catalina Mountains, and around Burro Creek Canyon.

Hutton's Vireo

Y

Habits:	Dense riparian growth along waterways at the lower elevations.
Chances:	Poor.
Key Sites:	Santa Cruz and San Pedro rivers, Guadalupe Canyon, Florida Wash, and San Simon Marsh.

Orange-crowned Warbler

W   B

Habits:	Brushy clearings, aspen groves, and forest undergrowth.
Chances:	Moderate.
Key Sites:	Organ Pipe Cactus National Monument, Saguaro National Monument, Buenos Aires National Wildlife Refuge, and Sabino Canyon.

 = Winter   = Year-round   = Breeding (Summer)

Virginia's Warbler

B

Habits: Brushy areas in the pine belt of higher elevations.

Chances: Poor.

Key Sites: Below Rustler Park, along the Crest Trail of the Huachucas and the roads of Mount Lemmon. Also farther north in the White Mountains and above the Mogollon Rim.

Lucy's Warbler

B

Habits: Summer resident of mesquite patches in the lower desert.

Chances: Moderate.

Key Sites: Guadalupe Canyon, Organ Pipe Cactus National Monument, lower Madera Canyon, Florida Wash, and San Xavier del Bac Mission south of Tucson.

Yellow-rumped Warbler

Habits: Summer resident of conifer forests of higher elevations.

Chances: Good.

Key Sites: Mounts Lemmon, Escudilla, Graham, and Wrightson, Rustler Park, Big Lake, and San Francisco Peaks.

Townsend's Warbler

W

Habits: Winters in coniferous forests. Also found in oak woodlands.

Chances: Poor.

Key Sites: Sky Islands, particularly Santa Rita and Huachuca mountains. Santa Gertrudis Road at Tumacacori, Patagonia Sonoita Creek Preserve, San Pedro River, and the San Simon Marsh.

 = Winter   = Year-round   = Breeding (Summer)

Grace's Warbler

B

Habits: Summer resident of open pine forests.

Chances: Good.

Key Sites: Mounts Lemmon, Wrightson, and Graham, near the San Francisco Peaks, higher peaks of the White Mountains, and Hualapai Peak.

MacGillivray's Warbler

B

Habits: Low, dense undergrowth and shady thickets. Small breeding colonies in state.

Chances: Poor.

Key Sites: San Francisco Peaks area and White Mountains along New Mexico border.

Red-faced Warbler

B

Habits: Summer resident of coniferous forests of higher elevations and oak forests just below. Look for in deciduous trees in pine forests.

Chances: Poor.

Key Sites: Pinery Canyon, Rustler Park, Mount Wrightson Trail in Madera Canyon, and Chiricahua Peak Trail.

Painted Redstart

B   Y

Habits: Summer resident of thick oak and pine-oak forests between 5,000 and 8,000 feet along streams.

Chances: Good.

Key Sites: All major canyons of the higher elevations in the Sky Islands.

 = Winter   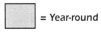 = Year-round    = Breeding (Summer)

Olive Warbler

Y

Habits:	Summer resident of coniferous forests at higher elevations.
Chances:	Moderate to Good.
Key Sites:	Mounts Lemmon and Wrightson, Miller Peak, and the Barfoot Lookout Trail out of Rustler Park.

Hepatic Tanager

B   Y

Habits:	Summer resident of thick oak woodlands and pine forests of Sky Islands.
Chances:	Good.
Key Sites:	Mount Lemmon, Madera Canyon, and most other major canyons in the Sky Islands.

Summer Tanager

B

Habits:	Summer resident of lower elevation riparian woodlands. Likes cottonwood.
Chances:	Good.
Key Sites:	Arivaca Creek in Buenos Aires National Wildlife Refuge, Empire/ Cienega Resource Conservation Area, Santa Cruz and San Pedro rivers, and Patagonia Sonoita Creek Preserve.

Western Tanager

B

Habits:	Summer resident of coniferous forests of higher elevations.
Chances:	Good.
Key Sites:	San Francisco Peaks area, Hualapai Peak, Mount Lemmon, Escudilla Mountain, and Mount Graham.

 = Winter   = Year-round   = Breeding (Summer)

Northern Cardinal

Y

Habits: Permanent resident of riparian woodlands and cities at lower elevations.

Chances: Good.

Key Sites: Arivaca Marsh, Guadalupe Canyon, along Santa Cruz and San Pedro rivers, Patagonia Sonita Creek Preserve, and Saguaro National Monument.

Pyrrhuloxia

Y

Habits: Permanent resident of dense brush, particularly mesquite, at lower elevations.

Chances: Good.

Key Sites: Anywhere from the San Pedro River west to Ajo.

Blue Grosbeak

B

Habits: Summer resident of riparian woodlands and brushy edges of irrigated fields.

Chances: Good.

Key Sites: San Pedro, Salt, and Santa Cruz rivers, Patagonia Sonoita Creek Preserve, San Simon Marsh, and marshlands of the White Mountains.

Lazuli Bunting

W   B

Habits: Spring and fall migrant of riparian thickets and tall weed patches. Breeds on northern plateaus.

Chances: Moderate to Good.

Key Sites: Anywhere west of San Pedro Valley for migration, and in the Four Corners region for breeding.

 = Winter   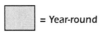 = Year-round   = Breeding (Summer)

Varied Bunting

B

Habits: Summer resident of dense mesquite patches.

Chances: Poor to Moderate.

Key Sites: Guadalupe Canyon, foothills of the Catalina Mountains, near Peña Blanca Lake, and south of Patagonia.

Green-tailed Towhee

W

B

Habits: Winter visitor to weedy fields and dense brush at lower elevations. Breeds on high plateaus in the northern portion of the state.

Chances: Moderate.

Key Sites: Sabino Canyon, Santa Cruz and San Pedro rivers, Guadalupe Canyon, and in pinyon-juniper forests of Navajo Reservation.

Canyon Towhee

Y

Habits: Arid brushlands, open chaparral, and pinyon-juniper forests.

Chances: Moderate.

Key Sites: Any of the major canyons of the Sky Islands, Mogollon Rim, and White Mountain regions.

Abert's Towhee

Y

Habits: Permanent resident of riparian woodlands and mesquite patches.

Chances: Poor.

Key Sites: Sabino Canyon, Organ Pipe Cactus National Monument, higher elevations in the small mountain ranges of the western portion of the state.

 = Winter    = Year-round   = Breeding (Summer)

Cassin's Sparrow

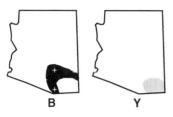

B   Y

Habits: Summer resident in grasslands with scattered bushes.

Chances: Moderate.

Key Sites: Lower canyons of the Sky Islands, Florida Wash, Empire Cienega Resource Conservation Area, Buenos Aires National Wildlife Refuge, and along AZ 181 west of Chiricahua National Monument.

Rufous-crowned Sparrow

Y

Habits: Permanent resident of grassy areas in open brushlands on rocky hillsides.

Chances: Good.

Key Sites: Guadalupe Canyon, Sabino Canyon, Florida Wash, and Peña Blanca Lake.

Brewer's Sparrow

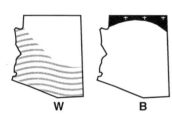

W   B

Habits: Winter visitor to open fields and open grasslands with brush.

Chances: Good.

Key Sites: Desert around Tucson and San Rafael, and San Pedro and Sulphur Springs valleys.

Black-chinned Sparrow

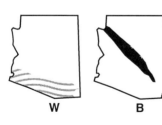

W   B

Habits: Permanent resident of brushy canyon slopes of Catalina and Chiricahua mountains.

Chances: Poor.

Key Sites: Sabino Canyon, Molino Basin, Tucson Sewage Ponds, and above dam in Lower Bear Canyon.

 = Winter    = Year-round   = Breeding (Summer)

Sage Sparrow

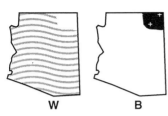

W   B

Habits: Permanent resident of dry hillsides, chaparral, and sagebrush. Winters in low desert.

Chances: Moderate.

Key Sites: Try canyons throughout the state.

Lark Bunting

W

Habits: Winter visitor to open deserts and grasslands.

Chances: Good.

Key Sites: Buenos Aires National Wildlife Refuge, Sulphur Springs Valley, Empire/ Cienega Resource Conservation Area, Organ Pipe Cactus National Monument, and fields along the Santa Cruz and San Pedro rivers.

Botteri's Sparrow

B

Habits: Summer residents of grasslands with scattered bushes.

Chances: Poor.

Key Sites: Buenos Aires National Wildlife Refuge, Empire/Cienega Resource Conservation Area, and around the foothills of the Santa Rita and Huachuca mountains.

Baird's Sparrow

W

Habits: Grasslands of higher elevations.

Chances: Poor.

Key Sites: Most common east of the Santa Rita Mountains, and at Peña Blanca Lake, near Patagonia Sonoita Creek Preserve and in Sulphur Springs Valley.

 = Winter   = Year-round   = Breeding (Summer)

Swamp Sparrow

W

Habits: Freshwater marshes with bushes and cattails.

Chances: Poor.

Key Sites: Guadalupe Canyon and any marshes from Douglas to the east.

Black-throated Sparrow

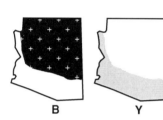

B   **Y**

Habits: Permanent resident of cactus and open brush at lower elevations.

Chances: Good.

Key Sites: Along San Pedro River, in Florida Wash, and Saguaro National Monument.

Yellow-headed Blackbird

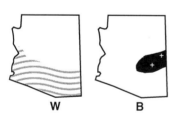

W   **B**

Habits: Winter visitor to water holes, cattle pens, and fields.

Chances: Good.

Key Sites: Irrigated fields along Santa Cruz and San Pedro rivers, Picacho Reservoir, Phon D. Sutton Wildlife Area, and Tucson Sewage Ponds.

Great-tailed Grackle

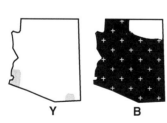

Y   **B**

Habits: Permanent resident anywhere near people. Also near ponds surrounded by trees at lower elevations.

Chances: Good.

Key Sites: City parks of Phoenix, Tucson, and smaller cities, and in farming areas along Santa Cruz and San Pedro rivers.

 = Winter   = Year-round   = Breeding (Summer)

Scott's Oriole

B   Y

Habits: Summer resident of oak and pine-oak woodlands, particularly where there is also yucca or agave.

Chances: Moderate.

Key Sites: Molino Basin, AZ 82 east of Sonoita, and in the mountain canyons of the Sky Islands.

Rosy Finch

Y

Habits: Permanent resident of rocky summits and snowfields.

Chances: Poor.

Key Sites: Mount Trumbull and other peaks along the high plateau north of the Grand Canyon.

Red Crossbill

Y

Habits: Permanent resident of coniferous forests of higher mountains.

Chances: Moderate.

Key Sites: Can be found in all the higher mountains of the state.

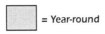 = Winter   = Year-round   = Breeding (Summer)

Reporting rare bird information

Amateurs make a significant contribution to the study of ornithology. Bird observations can only stand the test of time if they are thoroughly documented. Amateur birders are encouraged to submit written detailed information on bird distribution or interesting, rare, accidental, or unusual birds by contacting:

Arizona Bird Committee   or   Bird Sightings
4619 E. Arcadia Lane   Tucson Audubon Society
Phoenix, AZ 85018   300 E. University Boulevard
(no phone)   Tucson, AZ 85705
                                             (520) 629-0510

The Arizona Bird Committee requests precise details such as exact locality, optical equipment used, length of time bird observed, description (preferably made without the use of a field guide), basis you used for identification, your previous birding experience, and supporting evidence such as photographs and tape recordings when reporting rare species. You can obtain rare bird report forms from the committee by contacting one of the addresses above. A copy of the form is on the next two pages.

For casual reporting or obtaining immediate information about rare bird sightings call the Arizona Birding Hotlines in Maricopa Audubon Society, Phoenix; (602) 832-8745, or Tucson Audubon Society, Tucson; (520) 798-1005.

Arizona Bird Committee

VERIFICATION OF UNUSUAL SIGHT RECORD

SPECIES _____ DATE _____

NUMBER _____ AGE _____ SEX _____

LOCALITY _____
Exact address or other specific information to describe location, such as x miles
north of x intersection

COUNTY _____ CITY _____ ELEVATION _____

TIME _____ LENGTH OF TIME OBSERVED _____

HABITAT _____

DISTANCE TO BIRD _____ LIGHT CONDITIONS _____

OPTICAL EQUIPMENT _____

OBSERVER _____

OTHER OBSERVERS WHO INDEPENDENTLY IDENTIFIED THIS BIRD _____

_____

_____

Write a detailed description of the bird's appearance, including size, shape, plumage pattern,
color, and any unique features.

DESCRIPTION _____

_____

_____

_____

_____

_____

_____

_____

_____

_____

_____

_____

_____

_____

_____

_____

BEHAVIOR _____

_____

_____

_____

_____

VOICE AND/OR CALL NOTES _____

_____

_____

DESCRIBE WHAT SPECIFIC FEATURE(S) YOU SAW AND/OR HEARD
THAT CAUSED YOU TO COME TO YOUR CONCLUSIONS _____

_____

_____

_____

WHAT SIMILAR SPECIES MIGHT IT HAVE BEEN, AND HOW WERE THESE ELIMINATED?

_____

_____

_____

WHAT EXPERIENCE HAVE YOU HAD WITH THIS AND SIMILAR SPECIES?

_____

_____

_____

BOOKS, ILLUSTRATIONS, AND ADVICE CONSULTED,
AND HOW DID THESE INFLUENCE THIS DESCRIPTION? _____

_____

_____

SIGNIFICANCE OF RECORD IN THE AREA AND/OR THE STATE _____

_____

_____

ADDITIONAL MATERIAL (ATTACH DRAWING (DRAWINGS ENCOURAGED),
PHOTOGRAPH, TAPE RECORDING IF AVAILABLE) _____

_____

SIGNATURE _____

ADDRESS _____

DATE PREPARED _____

Arizona birding organizations

Huachuca Audubon Society, P.O. Box 63, Sierra Vista, AZ 85636

Maricopa Audubon Society, P.O. Box 15451, Phoenix, AZ 85060

Northern Arizona Audubon Society, P.O. 1496, Sedona, AZ 86336

Prescott Audubon Society, P.O. Box 4156, Prescott, AZ 86303

Tucson Audubon Society, 300 E. University Boulevard, Tucson, AZ 85705 (520) 629-0510

Yuma Audubon Society, P.O. Box 6395, Yuma, AZ 85366

Agency index

U.S. Department of the Interior

U.S. Fish and Wildlife Refuges

Bill Williams Delta National Wildlife Refuge
  60911 Highway 95, Parker, AZ 85344; (520) 667-4144

Buenos Aires National Wildlife Refuge
  P.O. Box 109, Sasabe, AZ 85633; (520) 823-4251

Cabeza Prieta National Wildlife Refuge
  1611 N. Second Avenue, Ajo, AZ 85321; (520) 387-6483

Imperial National Wildlife Refuge
  P.O. Box 72217, Yuma, AZ 85365; (520) 783-3371

Kofa National Wildlife Refuge
  356 W. 1st Street, P.O. Box 6290, Yuma, AZ 85366-6290;
  (520) 783-7861

San Bernadino National Wildlife Refuge
  1408 10th Street, Douglas, AZ 85607; (520) 364-2104

National Park Service

Canyon de Chelly National Monument
  P.O. Box 588, Chinle, AZ 86503; (520) 674-5500

Chiricahua National Monument
  Dos Cabezas Route, Box 6500, Willcox, AZ 85643; (520) 824-3560

Coronado National Memorial
  4101 E. Montezuma Canyon Road, Hereford, AZ 85615;
  (520) 366-5515

Sunset Crater National Monument
  2717 N. Steves Boulevard, #3 Flagstaff, AZ 86004; (520) 527-7042.
  Headquarters phone (520) 556-7134. Park is located 13 miles north of
  Flagstaff off Highway 89.

Walnut Canyon National Monument
  Walnut Canyon Road, Flagstaff, AZ 86004; (520) 526-3367. Park is
  located off I-40, 7.5 miles east of Flagstaff.

Wupatki National Monument
  2717 N. Steves Boulevard, #3 Flagstaff, AZ 86004; (520) 556-7040.
  Headquarters phone (520) 556-7134. Park is located 13 miles north of
  Flagstaff off Highway 89.

Glen Canyon National Recreation Area
P.O. Box 1507, Page, AZ 86040; (520) 608-6200

Grand Canyon National Park
P.O. Box 129, Grand Canyon, AZ 86023; (520) 638-7888

Montezuma Castle National Monument
P.O. Box 219, Camp Verde, AZ 86322; (520) 567-3322

Navajo National Monument
HC 71 Box 3, Tonalea, AZ 86044; (520) 672-2366 or 2367

Organ Pipe Cactus National Monument
Route 1, Box 100, Ajo, AZ 85321; (520) 387-6849

Petrified Forest National Park
P.O. Box 2217, Petrified Forest National Park, AZ 86028;
(520) 524-6228

Rainbow Bridge National Monument
c/o Glen Canyon NRA, P.O. Box 1507, Page AZ 86040; (520) 608-6200

Saguaro National Monument
36933 Old Spanish Trail, Tucson, AZ 85730-5699; (520) 733-5100

U.S. Department of Agriculture Forest Service

Apache-Sitgreaves National Forest

Apache-Sitgreaves National Forest Supervisor
P.O. Box 640, Springerville, AZ 85938; (520) 333-4301

Alpine Ranger District
P.O. Box 469, Alpine, AZ 85920; (520) 339-4384

Chevelon Ranger District
HC 62, Box 600, Winslow, AZ 86047; (520) 289-2471

Clifton Ranger District
P.O. Box 698, Clifton, AZ 85533; (520) 687-1301

Heber Ranger District
P.O. Box 968, Overgaard, AZ 85933; (520) 535-4481

Lakeside Ranger District,
RR 3, Box B-50, Lakeside, AZ 85929; (520) 368-5111

Springerville Ranger District
P.O. Box 760, Springerville, AZ 85938; (520) 333-4372

Coconino National Forest

Coconino National Forest Supervisor
2323 E. Greenlaw Lane, Flagstaff, AZ 86004; (520) 556-7400

Beaver Creek Ranger District
HC 64, Box 240, Rimrock, AZ 86335; (520) 567-4501

Blue Ridge Ranger District
HC 31, Box 300, Happy Jack, AZ 86024; (520) 477-2255

Long Valley Ranger District
HC 31, P.O. Box 68, Happy Jack, AZ 86024; (520) 354-2216

Mormon Lake Ranger District
4373 S. Lake Mary Rd., Flagstaff, AZ 86001; (520) 774-1182

Peaks Ranger District,
5075 N. Highway 89, Flagstaff, AZ 86004; (520) 526-0866

Sedona Ranger District
P.O. Box 300, Sedona AZ 86339-0300; (520) 282-4119

Coronado National Forest

Coronado National Forest Supervisor, Federal Building
300 W. Congress Street, Tucson, AZ 85701; (520) 670-4552

Douglas Ranger District
RR 1, Box 228-R, Douglas, AZ 85607; (520) 364-3468

Nogales Ranger District
2251 N. Grand Avenue, Nogales, AZ 85621; (520) 281-2296

Safford Ranger District
Post Office Building., 3rd Floor, P.O. Box 709, Safford, AZ 85548;
(520) 428-4150

Santa Catalina Ranger District,
5700 N. Sabino Canyon Road, Tucson, AZ 85750; (520) 749-8700

Sierra Vista Ranger District
5990 S. Highway 92, Hereford, AZ 85615; (520) 378-0311

Kaibab National Forest

Kaibab National Forest Supervisor
800 S. 6th Street, Williams, AZ 86046; (520) 635-8200.
Two visitor centers take all tourist calls for the four ranger districts
(Chalender, North Kaibab, Tusayan, and Williams) in this national
forest. They refer calls they can not handle:

Williams—Forest Service Visitor Center
200 W. Railroad Avenue, Williams, AZ 86046; (520) 635-4707

Kaibab Plateau Visitor Center
HC 64, Jacob Lake, AZ 86022; (520) 643-7298

Prescott National Forest

Prescott National Forest Supervisor
344 S. Cortez Street, Prescott, AZ 86303; (520) 445-1762

Bradshaw Ranger District
2230 E. Highway 69, Prescott, AZ 86301; (520) 445-7253

Chino Valley Ranger District
735 N. Highway 89, P.O. Box 485, Chino Valley, AZ 86323;
(520) 636-2302

Verde Ranger District
P.O. Box 670, Camp Verde, AZ 86322-0670; (520) 567-4121

Tonto National Forest

Tonto National Forest Supervisor
2324 E. McDowell Road, Phoenix, AZ 85006; (602) 225-5200

Cave Creek Ranger District
7171 E. Cave Creek Road, Carefree, AZ 85377; (602) 488-3441

Globe Ranger District
Route 1, Box 33, Globe, AZ 85501; (520) 425-7189

Mesa Ranger District
6 N. MacDonald Drive, Room 120, Mesa, AZ 85211; (602) 379-6446

Payson Ranger District
1009 East Highway 260, Payson, AZ 84451; (520) 474-7900

Pleasant Valley Ranger District
State Route 288, P.O. Box 450, Young, AZ 85554; (520) 462-3311

Tonto Basin Ranger District
Highway 88, P.O. Box 469, Roosevelt, AZ 85545; (520) 467-3200

Tonto Basin Visitor Center
Highway 88, P.O. Box 469, Roosevelt, AZ 85545; (520) 467-2234

Bureau of Land Managment

BLM Arizona State Office
3707 N. 7th Street, P.O. Box 16563, Phoenix, AZ 85011; (602) 650-0200

Arizona Strip District Office
390 North, 3050 East, St. George, UT 84770, (801) 673-3545

Shivwits and Vermillion Resource Areas
390 North, 3050 East, St. George, UT 84770; (801) 628-4491

Phoenix District Office
2015 W. Deer Valley Road, Phoenix, AZ 85027-2099; (602) 780-8090

Kingman Resource Area
2475 Beverly Avenue, Kingman, AZ 86401; (520) 757-3161

Lower Gila Resource Area
2015 W. Deer Valley Road, Phoenix, AZ 85027-2099; (602) 780-8090

Phoenix Resource Area
2015 W. Deer Valley Road, Phoenix, AZ 85027-2099; (602) 780-8090

Safford District Office
711 14th Avenue, Safford, AZ 85546-3321; (520) 428-4040

San Pedro Riparian National Conservation Area
1763 Paseo San Luis, Sierra Vista, AZ 85635; (520) 458-3559

Gila Resource Area
711 14th Avenue, Safford, AZ 85546-3321; (520) 428-4040

San Simon Resource Area
711 14th Avenue, Safford, AZ 85546-3321; (520) 428-4040

Yuma District Office
3150 Winsor Avenue, Yuma, AZ 85365-3594; (520) 726-6300

Havasu Resource Area
3189 Sweetwater Avenue, Lake Havasu City, AZ 86406-9071;
(520) 855-8017

Yuma Resource Area
3150 Winsor Avenue, Yuma, AZ 85365-3594; (520) 726-6300;
Las Cruces District Office, 1800 Marquess Street, Las Cruces, NM
88005; (505) 525-4300

Arizona Game & Fish Department

Arizona Game & Fish Department
  2221 W. Greenway Road, Phoenix, AZ 85023; (602) 942-3000

Region 1 Game & Fish
  HC 66, Box 57201, Pinetop, AZ 85935; (520) 367-4281
  Allen Severson Memorial Wildlife Area, Show Low Jacques Marsh
  Wildlife Area, Lakeside Springerville Marsh Wildlife Area, Springerville

Region 2 Game & Fish
  3500 S. Lake Mary Road, Flagstaff, AZ 86001; (520) 774-5045
  Chevelon Creek Wildlife Area, Winslow House Rock Wildlife Area,
  Flagstaff Raymond Ranch Wildlife Area, Flagstaff

Region 3 Game & Fish
  5325 N. Stockton Hill Road, Kingman, AZ 86401; (520) 692-7700

Region 4 Game & Fish
  9140 E. County, 10 1/2 Street, Yuma, AZ 85365; (520) 342-0091
  Mittry Lake Wildlife Area, Yuma

Region 5 Game & Fish
  555 N. Greasewood Road, Tucson, AZ 85745; (520) 628-5376
  Willcox Playa Wildlife Area, Willcox

Region 6 Game & Fish,
  7200 E. University Drive, Mesa, AZ 85207; (602) 981-9400
  Arlington Wildlife Area, Buckeye Base Meridian/Amator Wildlife Area,
  Phoenix Cluff Ranch Wildlife Area, Pima Robbins Butte Wildlife Area,
  Buckeye

Arizona State Parks

Arizona State Parks Board
  800 W. Washington, Suite 415, Phoenix, AZ 85007; (602) 542-4174

Arizona State Parks Public Information Officer
  1300 W. Washington Street, Phoenix, AZ 85007; (602) 542-1996

The Arizona state parks system includes a number of units with excellent
  birding opportunities. These publish checklists and offer guided bird
  walks throughout much of the year. Contact the parks you are interested
  in to find out what programs they have for birders.

Alamo Lake State Park
  P.O. Box 38, Wenden, AZ 85257; (520) 669-2066

Boyce Thompson Arboretum
P.O. Box AB, Superior, AZ 85273; (520) 689-2723

Buckskin Mountain State Park
P.O. Box BA, Parker, AZ 85344; (520) 667-3231

Catalina State Park
P.O. Box 36986, Tucson, AZ 85740; (520) 628-5798

Cattail Cove State Park
P.O. Box 1990, Lake Havasu City, AZ 86405; (520) 855-1223

Dead Horse Ranch State Park
P.O. Box 144, Cottonwood, AZ 86326; (520) 634-5263

Fool Hollow State Park
P.O. Box 2588, Show Low, AZ 85901; (520) 537-3680

Fort Verde State Park
P.O. Box 387, Camp Verde, AZ 86322; (520) 567-3275

Homolovi Ruins State Park
523 W. 2nd Street, Winslow, AZ 86947; (520) 289-4100

Jerome State Park
Box D, Jerome, AZ 86331; (520) 634-5381

Kartchner Caverns
P.O. Box 1849, Benson, AZ 85602; (520) 586-7257

Lake Havasu State Park
1350 W. McCullough Boulevard, Lake Havasu City, AZ 86406;
(520) 855-7851

Lost Dutchman State Park
6109 N. Apache Trail, Apache Junction, AZ 85219; (602) 982-4485

McFarland Historical State Park
P.O. Box 109, Florence, AZ 85232; (520) 866-5216

Oracle State Park
P.O. Box 700, Oracle, AZ 85623; (520) 896-2425

Patagonia Lake State Park
P.O. Box 274, Patagonia, AZ 85624: (520) 287-6965

Pichacho Peak State Park
P.O. Box 275, Pichacho Peak, AZ 85241; (520) 466-3183

Red Rock State Park
P.O. Box 3864, West Sedona, AZ 86340; (520) 282-8907

Riordan State Historical Park
    1300 Riordan Rancho Street, Flagstaff, AZ 86001; (520) 779-4395

Roper Lake State Park
    Route 2, Box 85546, Safford, AZ 85546; (520) 426-6760

Slide Rock State Park
    P.O. Box 10358, Sedona, AZ 86339; (520) 282-3034

Tombstone Courthouse State Park
    P.O. Box 216, Tombstone, AZ 85638; (520) 457-3311

Tonto Natural Bridge State Park
    P.O. Box 1245, Payson, AZ 85547; (520) 476-4202

Tubac Presidio State Park
    P.O. Box 274, Patagonia, AZ 85624; (520) 396-2252

The Nature Conservancy

TNC Arizona Field Office
    300 E. University Boulevard., Suite 230, Tucson, AZ 85705;
    (520) 622-3861

Aravaipa Canyon Preserve
    Klondyke Station, Willcox, AZ 85643; (520) 828-3443

Hassayampa River Preserve
    49614 Highway 60, P.O. Box 1162, Wickenburg, AZ 85358;
    (520) 684-2772

Muleshoe Ranch Cooperative Management Area
    RR 1, Box 1542, Willcox, AZ 85643; (520) 384-2626

Patagonia Sonoita Creek Preserve
    P.O. Box 815, Patagonia, AZ 85624; (520) 394-240

Ramsey Canyon Preserve
    RR1, Box 84, (27 Ramsey Canyon Road), Hereford, AZ 85615;
    (520) 378-2785

Miscellaneous Birding Areas

Hualapai Mountain Park
    Pine Lake Star Route, Kingman, AZ 86401; (520) 757-3859

Arizona-Sonora Desert Museum
    2021 North Kinney Road, Tucson, AZ 85743; (520) 883-1380

Maricopa County Parks and Recreation District
    3475 W. Durango Street, Phoenix, AZ 85009; (602) 506-2930

American Birding Association code of ethics

We, the Membership of the American Birding Association, believe that all birders have an obligation at all times to protect wildlife, the natural environment, and the rights of others. We therefore pledge ourselves to provide leadership in meeting this obligation by adhering to the following general guidelines of good birding behavior.

I. Birders must always act in ways that do not endanger the welfare of birds or other wildlife.

In keeping with this principle, we will:

Observe and photograph birds without knowingly disturbing them in any significant way.

Avoid chasing or repeatedly flushing birds. Only sparingly use recordings and similar methods of attracting birds and not use these methods in heavily birded areas.

Keep an appropriate distance from nests and nesting colonies so as not to disturb them or expose them to danger.

Refrain from handling birds or eggs unless engaged in recognized research activities.

II. Birders must always act in ways that do not harm the natural environment.

In keeping with this principle, we will:

Stay on existing roads, trails, and pathways whenever possible to avoid trampling or otherwise disturbing fragile habitat.

Leave all habitat as we found it.

III. Birders must always respect the rights of others.

In keeping with this principle, we will:

Respect the privacy and property of others by observing "No trespassing" signs and by asking permission to enter private or posted lands.

Observe all laws and the rules and regulations which govern public use of birding areas.

Practice common courtesy in our contacts with others. For example, we will limit our requests for information, and we will make them at reasonable hours of the day.

Always behave in a manner that will enhance the image of the birding community in the eyes of the public.

IV. Birders in groups should assume special responsibilities.

As group members, we will:

Take special care to alleviate the problems and disturbances that are multiplied when more people are present.

Act in consideration of the group's interest, as well as our own.

Support by our actions the responsibility of the group leader(s) for the conduct of the group.

As group leaders, we will:

Assume responsibility for the conduct of the group.

Learn and inform the group of any special rules, regulations, or conduct applicable to the area or habitat being visited.

Limit groups to a size that does not threaten the environment or the peace and tranquility of others.

Teach others birding ethics by our words and example.

Bibliography

Selected readings on Arizona birds

Alden, P. 1969. *Finding birds in Western Mexico.* Tucson, University of Arizona Press. (Out of print)

American Birding Association. 1982. *ABA checklist: Birds of Continental United States and Canada,* second ed. Austin, Texas.

American Ornithologists' Union. 1983. *Check-list of North American Birds,* sixth ed. Baltimore. American Ornithological Union. Additional supplements published in *The Auk* 1985, 1987, and 1989.

Clark, W. S., and B. K. Wheeler. 1987. *Field Guide to Hawks of North America.* Boston. Houghton Mifflin.

Cowgill, P., and E. Glendening. 1981. *Trail Guide to the Santa Catalina Mountains.* Tucson, Arizona. Rainbow Expeditions.

Davis, W. A., and S. M. Russell. 1990. *Birds in Southeastern Arizona.* Tucson, Arizona. Tucson Audubon Society.

Harrison, H. H. 1979. *A Field Guide to Birds' Nests in the Western U.S.* Boston. Houghton Mifflin.

Holt, H. R. 1989. *A Birder's Guide to Southeastern Arizona.* Colorado Springs, Colorado. American Birding Association.

Kaufman, K. 1990. *A Field Guide to Advanced Birding.* Boston. Houghton Mifflin.

Marshall, J. T., Jr. 1957. Birds of Pine-oak Woodland in Southern Arizona and Adjacent Mexico. *Pacific Coast Avifauna* 32:1-125.

Martin, R., and D. Martin. 1986. *Hiking Guide to the Santa Rita Mountains.* Boulder, Colorado. Pruett.

McMoran, C. W. 1981. *Hiking Trails of the Huachuca Mountains.* Sierra Vista, Arizona. Huachuca Mountain Publishers.

Monson, G., and A. R. Phillips. 1981. *Annotated Checklist of the Birds of Arizona,* second ed. Tucson. University of Arizona Press.

National Geographic Society. 1987. *Birds of North America,* second ed. National Geographic Society, Washington, DC.

Peterson. R. T. 1990. *A Field Guide to Western Birds,* third ed. Boston. Houghton Mifflin.

Peterson, R. T., and E. L. Chalif. 1973. *A Field Guide to Mexican Birds.* Boston. Houghton Mifflin.

Pettingill, O. S. 1981. *A Guide to Bird Finding,* volumes 1 and 2. New York. Oxford University Press.

Phillips, A., J. Marshall, and G. Monson. 1964. *The Birds of Arizona.* Tucson. University of Arizona Press.

Taylor, R. C. 1980. *The Coppery-tailed Trogon: Arizona's "Bird of Paradise."* Portal, Arizona. Borderland Productions. (Out of print)

Tyrrell, R., and E. Tyrell 1985. *Hummingbirds: Their Life and Behavior.* New York. Crown.

Udvardy, M. D. F. 1977. *The Audubon Society Field Guide to North American Birds,* Western ed. New York. Knopf.

Birding Magazines

American Birds, National Audubon Society, 950 Third Avenue, New York, NY 10022; (212) 832-3200. $27.50/year for 5 issues.

Bird Watcher's Digest, Box 110, Marietta, OH 45750; (800) 421-9764, 614-373-5285. $15/year for 6 issues.

Birder's World, 720 E. 8th Street, Holland, MI 49423; (616) 396-5618. $25/year for 6 issues.

Birding, American Birding Association, Box 4335, Austin, TX 78765. Free to members; $28/year for 6 issues for nonmembers.

The Auk, American Ornithologists' Union, c/o National Museum of Natural History, Washington, DC 20560; (202) 357-2051. $35/year for 4 issues, including membership.

WildBird Magazine, Box 57900, Los Angeles, CA 90057; (213) 385-2222. $27/year for 12 issues.

Index

Ajo 58
Alamo Lake 41–43
Allen Severson Wildlife Area 73–74
Alpine 77
American Birding Association ix, 5, 6, 196
Apache Junction 73
Apache Trail 71
Aravaipa Canyon 85–87
Arivaca 96
Arivaca Cienega 95
Arivaca Creek 94
Arizona Bird Committee viii, 10
Arizona Rare Bird Alert 6
Arizona-Sonora Desert Museum 92–94
Aubrey Cliffs 22
Aubrey Valley 22–23
Audubon Society 6, 187
Avocet, American 11, 105, 123

Bear Canyon 89
Becard, Rose-throated
    100, 101, 109, 111, 133, 164
Betty's Kitchen 50–51
Big Lake 75
Bill Williams Delta National Wildlife Refuge
    41–43
Bill Williams Gorge 41–43
Bill Williams River 43
Bisbee 102
Bittern
    American 115
    Least 115
Blackbird
    Brewer's 12, 149
    Red-winged 60, 75, 148
    Rusty 148
    Yellow-headed 11, 41, 73, 74,
        75, 148, 182
Bluebird
    Eastern 11, 137, 171
    Mountain 12, 63, 77, 137, 172
    Western 20, 64, 75, 137, 171
Bobolink 148
Bobwhite,
    Northern (Masked) 94, 122, 154
Bonita Creek 81–82
Booby
    Blue-footed 114
    Brown 114
Brant 117
Buenos Aires National Wildlife Refuge vii, 94–
    96, 181
Bufflehead 11, 119
Bull Pasture 56
Bunting 87
    Indigo 144
    Lark 101, 146, 181
    Lazuli 144, 178

Painted 145
Varied 11, 107, 111, 145, 179
Burro Creek 51–54
Bushtit 135

Cabeza Prieta National Wildlife Refuge 58
Canvasback 73, 118
Canyon Creek 64–66
Caracara, Crested 101, 121, 157
Cardinal, Northern
    11, 66, 71, 73, 96, 101, 144, 178
Carefree 66
Carr Canyon 103
Catalina State Park 87–89
Catbird, Gray 138
Cave Creek Canyon 84, 108–110
Central Mountains 1, 8, 59–82
Chat, Yellow-breasted 101, 110, 143
Chickadee
    Black-capped 12, 135
    Mexican 11, 13, 135, 169
    Mountain 12, 27, 31, 135, 169
Chiricahua Mountains vii, 109
Chiricahuan Desert 7
Chukar 11, 18, 19, 121, 154
Clifton 81
Coleman Lake 24–25
Colorado City 19
Colorado Plateau 12
Colorado River ix, 1, 7, 8, 10, 12, 47, 50
Coot, American 122
Cormorant 26
    Double-crested 41, 115
    Olivaceous 115
Coronado Trail 79
Cottonwood 60
Cowbird
    Bronzed 11, 54, 149
    Brown-headed 11, 149
Crane, Sandhill 11, 47, 105, 122
Creeper, Brown 31, 136
Crossbill, Red 12, 21, 108, 150, 183
Crow, American 12, 135, 168
Cuckoo, Yellow-billed
    11, 60, 73, 81, 101, 159
Curlew, Long-billed 124

Dead Horse Ranch State Park 60–61
Dickcissel 145
Dipper, American 12, 31, 51, 63, 64, 136
Douglas 108
Dove
    Common Ground 54, 100, 101, 107, 159
    Inca 10, 41, 51, 159
    Mourning 32
    White-winged 10, 39, 40, 41, 44, 45,
        89, 92, 107, 159
Dowitcher
    Long-billed 11, 125
    Short-billed 125
Duck 25, 50
    Black-bellied Whistling 116

Bufflehead 11, 119
Canvasback 73, 118
Fulvous Whistling 116
Gadwall 11, 73, 117
Goldeneye, Barrow's 119
Goldeneye, Common 11, 118
Mallard 10, 11, 73, *101*, 117
Merganser, Common 119
Merganser, Hooded 11, 119
Merganser, Red-breasted 119
Mexican 10, *101*, 117, 152
Oldsquaw 118
Pintail, Northern 73, 117
Redhead 10, 33, 73, 118, 152
Ring-necked 118
Ruddy 119
Scaup, Greater 11, 118, 152
Scaup, Lesser 118
Scoter, Black 118
Scoter, Surf 118
Scoter, White-winged 118
Shoveler, Northern 117
Teal, Blue-winged 73, 117
Teal, Cinnamon 73, 117
Teal, Green-winged 51, 73, 117
Wigeon, American 118
Wigeon, Eurasian 118
Wood 117
Dudleyville 85
Dunlin 125

Eagar 75, 77
Eagle
Bald 24, 25, 33, 60, 63, 66, 69, 71, 79, 119
Golden 20, 22, 28, 29, 35, 39, 44, 45, 121
Eagle Creek 79–81
Egret 41, 50
Cattle 11, 116
Great 115
Reddish 115
Snowy 47, 115
Empire/Cienega Resource Conservation Area 110, 181
Escudilla Mountain 77–78
Estes Canyon 56

Fairbank 102
Falcon
Peregrine 33, 85, 121
Prairie
16, 20, 22, 28, 29, 33, 35, 39, 45, 60, 108, 121, 157
Finch
Cassin's 150
House 150
Purple 150
Rosy 12, 13, 18, 20, 149, 183
Fish Creek 71–73
Flagstaff 8, 29, 31, 33

Flicker
Northern (Gilded) 12, 18, 20, 27, 38, 54, 79, 92, 131
Red-shafted 131
Yellow-shafted 131
Florida Wash 97–100
Flycatcher 111
Ash-throated 11, 18, 20, 41, 133, 165
Brown-crested 89
Brown-crowned 133
Buff-breasted 11, 103, 132
Cordilleran 54, 57, 90
Dusky-capped 11, 132, 166
Gray 132
Hammond's 132
Least 132
Olive-sided 131
Scissor-tailed 133
Sulphur-bellied 11, 97, 108, 133, 165
Vermilion
11, 51, 54, 62, 66, 73, 91, 94, 96, 100, 132, 166
Western 27, 132
Willow 132
Fredonia 18
Frigatebird, Magnificent 115

Gadwall 11, 73, 117
Galiuro Mountains 85
Gallinule, Purple 122
Gila Box Riparian National Conservation Area 81
Gila River 81
Gnatcatcher 44, 45
Black-capped 137
Black-tailed 11, 66, 137, 171
Blue-gray 137
Godwit, Marbled 124
Goldeneye
Barrow's 119
Common 11, 118
Goldfinch
American 150
Lawrence's 150
Lesser 89, 150
Goose
Canada 41, 47, 71, 75, 117
Great White-fronted 116
Ross' 117
Snow 41, 47, 116
Goshawk, Northern 11, 20, 21, 77, 120
Grackle, Great-tailed 11, 149, 182
Grand Canyon National Park
North Rim 19, 20–22
South Rim 27
Grand Canyon Caverns 22
Grandview Point 27–29
Great Basin Desert 7
Grebe
Clark's 41
Eared 11, 33, 47, 114, 152
Horned 114

Least 114
Pied-billed 50, 114
Western 11, 114
Green Valley 100
Grosbeak
    Black-headed 107, 144
    Blue
        11, 41, 85, 87, 100, 101, 107, 108,
        144, 178
    Evening 12, 150
    Pine 12, 149
    Rose-breasted 144
    Yellow *106*, *107*, 144
Grouse, Blue 11, 21, 77, 121, 154
Guadalupe Canyon 107–108
Gull
    Bonaparte's 126
    California 126
    Franklin's 10, 125
    Glaucous-winged 126
    Heermann's 126
    Herring 11, 126
    Ring-billed 126
    Sabine's 126
    Thayer's 126

Harrier, Northern 10, 120
Hassayampa River Preserve 9, 51–54
Hawk 106
    Broad-winged 120
    Common Black 51, 63, 81, 85, 120, 156
    Cooper's 54, 107, 120
    Ferruginous 11, 22, 35, 39, 121, 157
    Gray 10, 53, 85, 94, 96, 100,
        101, 110, 120, 156
    Harris' 10, 11, 50, 51, 54, 66, 69, 71,
        91, 120, 156
    Red-shouldered 120
    Red-tailed
        20, 28, 29, 45, 66, 70, 71, 79, 81, 120
    Rough-legged 121
    Sharp-shinned 11, 41, 51, 53, 120
    Swainson's 11, 82, 94, 101, 120, 156
    Zone-tailed 10, 51, 53,
        81, 85, 90, 107, 120, 157
Heber 66
Hereford 102
Heron
    Black-crowned Night 51, 73, 116
    Great Blue
        47, 50, 51, 60, 66, 73, 75, 79,
        100, 110, 115
    Green-backed 50, 116
    Little Blue 115
    Tricolored 115
Holbrook 35
Honeymoon Campground 79–81
Horseshoe Dam 66–67
Huachuca Mountains vii, 181
Hualapai Mountain Park 39–40
Hummingbird 79, 97, 103, 109
    Allen's 10, 130

Anna's 11, 51, 129, 161
Berylline 129
Black-chinned 64, *104*, 129, 161
Blue-throated 10, 129
Broad-billed 10, 128
Broad-tailed 64, 77, *104*, 129, 162
Calliope 129
Costa's 11, 129, 162
Lucifer 129, 162
Magnificent 10, *104*, 129, 162
Rufous 64, 129
Violet-crowned 10, 107, 129
White-eared 128

Ibis
    White 116
    White-faced 116
Imperial National Wildlife Refuge vii, 13, 47–
    50, 152

J. D. Lake 26
Jacob Lake 21, 22
Jacques Marsh 73–74, 152
Jaeger
    Long-tailed 125
    Parasitic 125
    Pomarine 125
Jay 25
    Gray 12, 134, 167
    Gray-breasted
        11, 100, 107, 108, 134, 168
    Pinyon 12, 18, 19, 22, 27, 29, 134, 168
    Scrub 12, 51, 107, 134
    Steller's 12, 20, 21, 25, 33, 134, 167
Junco
    Dark-eyed 78, 100, 147, 148
    Gray-headed 12
    Slate-colored 147
    White-winged 147
    Yellow-eyed 11, 90, 108, 148

Kaibab Plateau 20–22
Kaibab squirrel 21
Kestrel, American 81, 121
Killdeer 12, 24, 25, 73, 74, 123
Kingbird
    Cassin's 100, 133, 165
    Eastern 133
    Thick-billed 11, 100, 107, 133, 165
    Tropical 11, 94, 133
    Western 100, 133
Kingfisher
    Belted 10, 24, 25, 60, 73, 74, 75, 130
    Green 10, 101, 110, 130, 163
Kinglet
    Golden-crowned 12, 137
    Ruby-crowned 137
Kingman 39, 51
Kingman Resource Area 54
Kite
    Black-shouldered 119

Mississippi 10, 51, 53,
    85, 101, 119, 155
  White-tailed 10, 110
Kittiwake, Black-legged 126
Knot, Red 124
Kofa National Wildlife Refuge vii, 44–45
Kohl's Ranch 66

Lake Havasu 43, 152
Lamar Haines Memorial Wildlife Area 31–32
Lark, Horned 12, 33, 35, 75, 94, 133
Little Colorado River 7, 8, 152
Longspur
  Chestnut-colored 148
  Lapland 148
  McCown's 11, 148
Loon
  Arctic 114
  Common 114
  Red-throated 114
Lukeville 58

Madera Canyon 97–100
Magpie, Black-billed 12, 135
Mallard 10, 11, 73, 101, 117
Martin, Purple 133
Martinez Lake 47–50, 152
Meadowlark
  Eastern 148
  Western 148
Merganser
  Common 119
  Hooded 11, 119
  Red-breasted 119
Merlin 10, 121
Mittry Lake 50–51, 152
Mockingbird, Northern 138
Mogollon Rim 7, 64
Mojave Desert 7
Moorhen, Common 122
Morenci 81
Mormon Lake 33–35
Mount Graham 10
Mount Lemmon 8, 9, 90
Mount Trumbull 18–20, 21

Navajo Reservation 36
Nighthawk
    Common 10, 33, 128, 160
    Lesser 10, 33, 41, 128, 160
Nightjar, Buff-collared
    10, 85, 86, 87, 97, 107, 128, 151,
    161
Nixon Springs 20
Nogales 100, 111
Northern Arizona 17-36
Nutcracker, Clark's 9, 12, 21, 25, 135, 168
Nuthatch
  Pygmy 27, 90, 136
  Red-breasted 31, 136
  White-breasted 18, 31, 136

Oak Creek Canyon 60
Oldsquaw 118
Organ Pipe Cactus National Monument
    vii, 54–58, 181
Oriole
  Baltimore. See Oriole, Northern
  Bullock's 149. See also Oriole, Northern
  Hooded 39, 44, 45,
    51, 54, 62, 89, 97, 108, 149
  Northern 62, 66, 97, 149
  Orchard 149
  Scott's 39, 45, 62, 89, 90, 91, 97,
    108, 149, 183
  Streak-backed 149
Osprey 25, 33, 60, 69, 71, 119
Ovenbird 142
Owl
  Barn 101
  Burrowing 105, 110, 127
  Elf 10, 38, 54, 87, 89, 92, 97, 127, 158
  Ferruginous Pygmy 127
  Flammulated
    10, 12, 33, 39, 97, 127, 158
  Great Horned 18, 39, 66, 67, 127
  Long-eared 127
  Northern Pygmy 12, 25, 127
  Northern Saw-whet 12, 27, 33, 128
  Short-eared 10, 128
  Spotted 12, 25, 34, 39, 127, 158
  Western Screech 34, 38, 39, 51, 91, 92,
    108, 127
  Whiskered Screech 10, 34, 38,
    97, 108, 127

Painted Desert 35
Palm Canyon 44, 45, 46
Parker 43
Parula, Northern 141
Patagonia 101
Patagonia Sonoita Creek Preserve 100–101,
    181
Payson 63, 66
Peach Springs 23
Pelican
  American White 41, 47, 114
  Brown 115
Peña Blanca Lake 111, 181
Petrified Forest National Park 35–36
Pewee
  Greater 90, 131
  Western Wood 131
Phainopepla 41, 44, 45,
    50, 54, 69, 73, 89, 91, 97, 139, 173
Phalarope
  Red 125
  Red-necked 125
  Wilson's 125
Pheasant, Ring-necked 11, 121
Phoebe
  Black 11, 47, 108, 132, 166
  Eastern 132

Say's 132, 166
Phoenix 8, 12, 51, 66
Phon D. Sutton Recreation Area 69–71
Pigeon, Band-tailed
    12, 33, 97, 100, 108, 158
Pine Canyon 63
Pinetop 73
Pintail, Northern 73, 117
Pipit
    Sprague's 139
    Water 139
Plover
    Black-bellied 123
    Lesser Golden 123
    Mountain 11, 105, 123, 153
    Semipalmated 123
    Snowy 123
Poorwill, Common 54, 97, 108, 128
Portal 109
Pronghorn 18, 19
Pyrrhuloxia 11, 54, 73, 87, 88, 89, 91,
    97, 144, 178

Quail
Gambel's
    11, 25, 27, 29, 33, 39, 43, 47, 51, 60,
    69, 71, 81, 90, 94, 122, 155
Montezuma
    10, 11, 94, 109, 110, 122, 151, 154
Scaled
    10, 12, 35, 94, 97, 101, 102, 122, 155
Quartzsite 44
Quitobaquito Springs 56

Rail
    Black 11, 122, 153
    Clapper 11, 122, 153
    Virginia 11, 122
    Yuma Clapper 47, 50
Ramsey Canyon 100, 103
Raven
    Chihuahuan 11, 105, 135, 169
    Common 23, 29, 112, 135
Red Butte 29–31
Red Mountain 29
Red Rock Country 7-8
Red Rock State Park 62–63
Redhead 10, 33, 73, 118, 152
Redstart
    American 142
    Painted 11, 90, 97, 108, 143, 176
Rincon Mountain 92
Rio Rico 111
Roadrunner, Greater
    10, 35, 39, 44, 45, 54, 89, 91, 151,
    160
Robin
    American 62, 138
    Rufous-backed 138
Roosevelt 71
Roosevelt Lake Wildlife Area 71–73
Rustler Park 108–110

Sabino Canyon Recreation Area 89
Safford 81, 86
Saguaro National Monument 91–92
Salt River 69, 71
San Francisco Peaks 8, 9, 31
San Pedro Riparian National Conservation
    Area vii, 9, 101–102
San Pedro River 101, 152, 181
San Simon Marsh 152
San Xavier del Bac Mission 96
Sanderling 11, 124
Sandpiper
    Baird's 124
    Least 47, 124
    Pectoral 124
    Semipalmated 124
    Solitary 10, 123
    Spotted 10, 12, 47, 124
    Stilt 125
    Western 47, 124
Sanata Cruz River 181
Santa Rita Lodge 97, 99
Santa Rita Mountains vii, 181
Sapsucker
    Red-breasted 130
    Red-naped 64. See Sapsucker: Yellow-
        bellied
    Williamson's 21, 130, 164
    Yellow-bellied 12, 100, 130
Sasabe 96
Scaup
    Greater 11, 118, 152
    Lesser 118
Scoter
    Black 118
    Surf 118
    White-winged 118
Sedona 63
Seligman 22
Shivwits Plateau vii
Shoveler, Northern 117
Show Low 73
Shrike
    Loggerhead 139
    Northern 139
Sierra Vista 102, 103
Siskin, Pine 12, 150
Sky Islands vii, 1, 7, 8, 9, 10, 12,
    83-112
Snipe, Common 12, 125
Solitaire, Townsend's 12, 137
Sonoita 101, 110
Sonoita Creek 100–101
Sonoran Desert ix, 1, 7, 8, 66, 73, 87, 92
Sora 122
Southwestern Research Station 109
Sparrow
    American Tree 145
    Baird's 11, 146, 181
    Black-chinned 146, 180
    Black-throated 146, 182
    Botteri's 11, 94, 145, 181

Brewer's 146, 180
Cassin's 11, 94, 145, 180
Chipping 12, 18, 20, 35, 97, 146
Clay-colored 146
Five-striped 111, 146
Fox 147
Golden-crowned 147
Grasshopper 11, 94, 147
Harris' 147
House 150
Lark 146
Lincoln's 100, 147
Rufous-crowned 87, 145, 180
Rufous-winged 11, 91, 97, 145
Sage 105, 146, 181
Savannah 146
Song 147
Swamp 147, 182
Vesper 146
White-crowned 147
White-throated 147
Spoffords' backyard 109
Spoonbill, Roseate 11, 116
Springerville 75–76, 76
Stargo 81
Starling, European 139
Starthroat, Plain-capped 129
Stilt, Black-necked 11, 123
Stork, Wood 10, 116
Sulphur Springs Valley 181
Summerhaven 90
Superstition Mountains 71
Swallow
    Bank 134
    Barn 134
    Cave 134
    Cliff 33, 35, 44, 45, 134
    Northern Rough-winged 54, 134
    Tree 11, 134, 167
    Violet-green 134
Swan, Tundra 116
Swift
    Chimney 128
    White-throated 89, 90, 128, 161
Sycamore Canyon 111–112

Tanager
    Hepatic 11, 97, 108, 144, 177
    Scarlet 11, 144
    Summer 11, 81, 94, 96, 97, 100,
        101, 107, 144, 177
    Western 12, 18, 35, 62, 77, 144, 177
Teal
    Blue-winged 73, 117
    Cinnamon 73, 117
    Green-winged 51, 73, 117
Tern
    Artic 126
    Caspian 11, 126
    Common 11, 126
    Forster's 10, 127
    Least 127

Terry Flat 77–78
Thrasher 45
    Bendire's 11, 35, 87, 96, 138, 172
    Brown 138
    Crissal
        11, 51, 87, 89, 91, 96, 97, 138, 173
    Curve-billed
        11, 39, 42, 43, 71, 89, 91, 138, 173
    Le Conte's 11, 139, 173
    Sage 12, 35, 44, 45, 91, 138, 172
Thrush
    Aztec 138
    Hermit 137
    Swainson's 12, 137
    Varied 138
    Wood 138
Titmouse
    Bridled 11, 90, 97, 100, 135, 169
    Plain 12, 135
Tombstone 102
Tonto Creek 64–66
Tonto Natural Bridge State Park 63
Topock Marsh 152
Tortilla Flat 73
Towhee
    Abert's 11, 50, 145, 179
    Brown 44, 45, 145
    Canyon 179
    Green-tailed 12, 54, 100, 145, 179
    Rufous-sided 145
Trogon
    Eared 130
    Elegant 10, 13, 97, 108, 111, 130, 151,
        163
Tucson 1, 8, 12, 85, 88, 89, 90, 92,
        93, 108
Tucson Mountain 92
Turkey, Wild 11, 18, 20,
        21, 24, 25, 28, 64, 77, 121
Turnstone, Ruddy 124
Tusayan 27, 29, 31
Tuvasci Marsh 60–61
Tuweep 19
Tyrannulet, Northern Beardless
        11, 85, 87, 97, 101, 131, 167

Uinkaret Plateau vii

Valle 31
Veery 12, 137, 172
Verde River 60, 66–67, 69
Verdin
        11, 41, 51, 54, 66, 91, 100, 135, 170
Vermillion Resource Area 20
Vireo
    Bell's 63, 85, 91, 97, 139, 174
    Gray 139, 174
    Hutton's 11, 140, 174
    Philadelphia 140
    Red-eyed 140
    Solitary 139, 140
    Warbling 140

Yellow-green 140
Yellow-throated 140
Vulture
Black 11, 54, 57, 119, 155
Turkey 11, 23, 119

Wabayuma Peak Wilderness 39–40
Warbler 25, 41, 62, 69
Audubon's 141
Bay-breasted 142
Black and White 142
Black-throated Blue 141
Black-throated Gray 141
Black-throated Green 141
Blackburnian 142
Blackpoll 142
Canada 143
Chestnut-sided 141
Golden-winged 140
Grace's 11, 21, 108, 142, 176
Hermit 141
Hooded 143
Kentucky 11, 143
Lucy's 54, 87, 92, 141, 175
MacGillivray's 143, 176
Magnolia 141
Myrtle 141
Nashville 140
Olive 11, 103, 143, 177
Orange-crowned 50, 90, 140, 174
Palm 142
Prairie 142
Prothonotary 142
Red-faced 90, 103, 108, 143, 176
Tennessee 140
Townsend's 141, 175
Virginia's 90, 108, 140, 175
Wilson's 143
Worm-eating 142
Yellow 85, 141
Yellow-rumped 50, 64, 77, 141, 175
Yellow-throated 142
Waterfowl 25, 34, 43, 47, 52, 60, 73, 76
Waterthrush
Louisiana 112, 143
Northern 143
Waxwing
Bohemian 139
Cedar 139
Western Arizona 37-58
Whimbrel 124
Whip-poor-will 10, 97, 128, 160
White Horse Lake 25–26
White Mountains 8, 9, 73, 75, 152
Why 58
Wickenburg 51
Wigeon
American 118
Eurasian 118
Wikieup 52
Willcox Playa Wildlife Area 105–106
Willet 10, 123

Williams 24, 26, 31
Wood-Pewee, Western 35, 51
Woodpecker 21, 25
Acorn 12, 25, 64, 65, 107, 108, 130
Downy 31, 63, 131
Gila 10, 38, 41, 71, 89, 92, 93,
107, 130, 163
Gilded 91
Hairy 10, 12, 27, 31, 39, 108, 131
Ladder-backed 10, 39, 41, 51, 89, 101,
107, 108, 131, 164
Lewis' 12, 25, 31, 130, 163
Strickland's 10, 90, 103, 108, 131
Three-toed 12, 27, 31, 64, 131, 164
Wren
Bewick's 100, 136, 170
Cactus 11, 51, 53, 54, 69, 71,
87, 89, 92, 136, 170
Canyon 44, 45,
54, 63, 81, 89, 136, 170
House 136
Long-billed Marsh 54
Marsh 11, 47, 60, 136
Rock 34, 54, 89, 136
Winter 136, 171

Yellowlegs
Greater 11, 123, 153
Lesser 123
Yellowthroat, Common 11, 143
Yuma 50